Praise for **DREAM GUIDANCE**

'In this very accessible book, Machiel Klerk explains the brass tacks of dream incubation. The how-to and the why, the history and the ancestry. Dream incubation gives us access to healing and creativity. It was just waiting for a simple—though not simplistic—guide. Here it is.'
— **Robert Bosnak**, author of *A Little Course in Dreams*

'Dream Guidance *offers an easy, open, and effective approach to engaging our inner wisdom and its advice! If you are looking for a way to connect with dreaming and your deeper self, try these incubation practices and discover your own dream guidance.*'
— **Robert Waggoner**, author of *Lucid Dreaming*

'Dreams respond as oracles, offering guidance to one of life's most precious treasures—the Soul. Few know the ways of connecting to these oracular powers. Machiel Klerk offers a step-by-step process of asking the focused questions that unleash the guiding wisdom of dreams. This book breaks new ground, opens new possibilities, speaks to the heart and soul. It is a must-read for those following the way of the dream.'
— **Dr Stephen Aizenstat PhD**, founder of Pacifica Graduate Institute and Dream Tending

'Dream Guidance *offers a rich resource of ideas and practices for incubating, working with, and learning from dreams. Machiel Klerk serves as a knowing guide as he draws knowledge from ancient practices and Indigenous healers to psychology and his own compelling insights into the wondrous realm of dreams.*'
— **Michael Meade**, author of *Awakening the Soul*

'Machiel Klerk has written a remarkable book on dreams. You will learn much from him how to make dreams a part of life. The book is clear and lively and doesn't get stuck in minor arguments and subtle the___ ___ ___
You need to make dreams a pa___
this book is a helpful guic___
— **Thomas Moore**, autho___

D1454648

DREAM GUIDANCE

DREAM GUIDANCE

CONNECTING TO THE SOUL
THROUGH DREAM INCUBATION

———

MACHIEL KLERK

HAY HOUSE

Carlsbad, California • New York City
London • Sydney • New Delhi

Published in the United Kingdom by:
Hay House UK Ltd, The Sixth Floor, Watson House,
54 Baker Street, London W1U 7BU
Tel: +44 (0)20 3927 7290; Fax: +44 (0)20 3927 7291; www.hayhouse.co.uk

Published in the United States of America by:
Hay House Inc., PO Box 5100, Carlsbad, CA 92018-5100
Tel: (1) 760 431 7695 or (800) 654 5126
Fax: (1) 760 431 6948 or (800) 650 5115; www.hayhouse.com

Published in Australia by:
Hay House Australia Ltd, 18/36 Ralph St, Alexandria NSW 2015
Tel: (61) 2 9669 4299; Fax: (61) 2 9669 4144; www.hayhouse.com.au

Published in India by:
Hay House Publishers India, Muskaan Complex, Plot No.3, B-2,
Vasant Kunj, New Delhi 110 070
Tel: (91) 11 4176 1620; Fax: (91) 11 4176 1630; www.hayhouse.co.in

Text © Machiel Klerk, 2022

Project editor: Anna Cooperberg
Cover design: Micah Kandros
Interior design: Karim J. Garcia

A catalogue record for this book is available from the British Library.

Tradepaper ISBN: 978-1-78817-794-8
E-book ISBN: 978-1-4019-6820-5
Audiobook ISBN: 978-1-4019-6821-2

MIX
Paper from
responsible sources
FSC® C013056

Printed and bound in Great Britain by
TJ Books Limited, Padstow, Cornwall

*To the world of dream and
its guiding inhabitants*

CONTENTS

INTRODUCTION

When I was lost, dreams were what guided me back home. It started in my early twenties, when I had entered into a grim one-way street in my life. I had not dealt well with the grief and loss of my father's death when I was 10. This, and other issues, had led to a meaningless and purposeless existence. By chance I stumbled upon the works of Carl Jung, which introduced me to the marvelous, magical, and life-enhancing world of dream.

After that, dreams started to show me where I was in life and gave me direction for the future. Dreams connected me in a wild and gentle way to my father, and to my vocation. Life became exciting again, full of meaning, color, and purpose. From then on, dreams became my passion, and I have been studying them ever since.

By now, I have filled dozens of dream diaries. I have read almost every book on dreams that I have been able to find, and have worked with dream therapists, shamans, and Jungian analysts.

In my early thirties, my fascination with dreams led me to complete a master's degree in counseling psychology with an emphasis on depth psychology at Pacifica Graduate Institute. Depth psychology is a tradition that takes the importance of dreams into account.

After my master's degree, I participated in a three-year training program to learn Embodied Imagination, a way of working with dreams developed by Robert Bosnak. I have worked as a mental health therapist since 2006, which has led me to hear and interpret about 20,000 of my patients' dreams.

Now I travel all over the world to talk to people about how to harness the power of their dreams. I have facilitated workshops on dreams in Africa, Europe, and North America. At one time I backpacked for a year through Asia, and in every country I visited, I learned their local way of being with dreams. I traveled to Africa and learned how African shamans worked with dreams. Through all my studies, I learned that there is not one best way to be with dreams; rather, there are many insightful techniques, tools, and perspectives. One can interpret a dream, feel and learn from emotions in a dream, relate and talk to dream figures, become lucid in the dream (and in a conscious way explore the dream environment), and finally, ask the dream a question before you fall asleep. Then you will receive a response from the dream. This book will deal mainly with that last subject.

Personally, my life is much richer due to being in touch with the world of dream. Dreams have helped me get over freezing up when I felt overwhelmed, encouraged me to take on a certain project, and have even notified me of upcoming deaths of loved ones.

In 2009 I had an important vocational dream. I am floating above Lake Zürich, looking over Carl Jung's house. The lake and dock are behind his house, next to his yard, and in the dream, there is a square concrete platform attached to the dock. Jung is in his late 60s or early 70s and is working on that platform, rearranging some beams to create a homier structure. Then he sits down on a chair and begins to read a book. At that moment, the image stops, turns black and white, and Jung and the platform disappear. A voice behind me says, "You have to draw this scene identically to how it was." I don't consider myself artistic, yet I find myself with a pencil in my hand. I make a line, straighter than I thought I could draw. And with that, I wake up. I took this dream as a suggestion to create a platform for Jung and soul-centered psychology. We are not in Jung's yard—we are in an extension of his yard. I took that as a suggestion not to follow Jung dogmatically but to build upon his work and continue exploring, just as Jung explored all kinds of spiritual traditions. This dream led me to start the Jung Society of Utah, and later on the online educational organization the Jung Platform.

As you can see, dreamwork has always been a practical tool for me. It's not an airy, abstract activity. What you discover through your dreams can serve as an impetus to act, which has a direct beneficial effect on your day-to-day life.

HOW I STARTED TO EXPLORE ASKING THE DREAM QUESTIONS

A decade ago, I had a long and intense lucid dream—a dream in which you know that you are dreaming—where I asked dream figures questions and made requests. I got some stunning and helpful responses from the dream figures. After that, I started to experiment with ways to ask the dream questions before I went to sleep, then see how the dream would respond. I spent a year and a half just testing, seeing what worked and what didn't, and also collaborated with my sister, who loves working with dreams.

I asked questions about my health, creativity, finances, business ventures, relationship challenges, and how to find love. I tried asking questions to mountains and trees and rivers. I wondered if dreams could predict the future, and what dreams could tell me about existential topics such as death and karma.

After my own exploration, I started to read every book I could find on the topic of asking your dreams questions, which is known as "dream incubation." I made pilgrimages to ancient Greek and Turkish temples where dream incubation had been a common healing practice for over a thousand years. I talked with Indigenous healers in Indonesia, Africa, and North America. From my own experience, from working with dreamers all over the world and learning from all these traditions, I distilled a working formula of five steps, which you will learn about in this book, to effective dream incubation.

I wrote this book because I felt gratitude toward the world of dream, and for all its guidance. I hope that these techniques will help you foster a closer relationship with your own dreams and help you feel happier and more fulfilled. In a literal sense, embodying your dream insights and living them in this reality will help you live a dream life.

CHAPTER 1

ASKING YOUR DREAM FOR HELP

Manuela is a young woman in her early 20s who attended a dream lecture I hosted in the Netherlands. Prior to her attending, she was unfamiliar with the concept of asking her dreams for guidance in her waking life. During the lecture, she said, "Recently, I've had problems with the amount of stress I experience in my life, and I often feel tired and restless." She explained that she had been seeking help for her troubles through a Traditional Chinese medicine healer, but that so far nothing had relieved her stress. That evening, after learning my dream technique, she went home and decided to ask her dreams: "Why do I experience stress so quickly?"

The next morning, I received an e-mail from her describing the dream response she experienced after asking that question. She said, "I see a woman with tattoos covering her entire body. She appears bold and is very muscular. She looks at me and then motions, pointing her finger toward the ocean. When I turn to look in the direction she is pointing, I see the glittering surface of the ocean, but I also see all the currents running beneath it.

The currents appear as different colors and different lights, which strikes me as bizarre. I walk over to the water and start to swim. The moment I give myself over to the current, the water carries me, and I don't have to do anything, and I am not struggling to stay afloat. This newfound feeling of relaxation is really great! However, I find that if I try to swim in a different direction and move against the current, I become exhausted with the struggle, and I begin to feel very stressed and scared of drowning."

This is a beautiful example of a dream incubation response that is fairly easy to interpret. The metaphor presented in Manuela's dream helped her realize that her stress level was dependent upon whether she allowed herself to "stay in the flow" and not struggle against the natural current of her life. Manuela didn't have much previous experience working with dreams, but she was still able to get a clear message. After reflecting on her dream, she felt excited and relieved to have received so much clarity around an issue that had been creating problems in her life.

Manuela's experience perfectly describes the process of dream incubation. It's a simple and ancient practice that has almost been forgotten in our modern world. Out of my work studying the history of dreaming as it relates to psychology, I've been able to distill a practical five-step method for accessing the power of your dreams. Manuela's experience illustrates these steps. First, she identified a problem that she'd like to fix and decided to proactively ask her dreams for help. Second, she developed a good question that related directly to that issue. Third, she engaged in a ritual to enhance the dream response. She did this by meditating on the question while she laid in bed. Fourth, she went to sleep, had a dream, woke up, and immediately recorded the dream. Fifth, she reflected on the dream, and actively implemented the "lesson" when she noticed anxiety creeping into her emotional state. She was able to remind herself of the peaceful experience in her dream when she allowed the current to keep her afloat. And when she felt stress, she asked herself if she's swimming against the current.

The goal of this book is to help you access the power of your own dreams, just like Manuela did. I hope to show you that the dreamworld wants to engage with you in order to provide answers to your most meaningful questions. Anyone can use my five-step method for proactively engaging with their dreams, and the result can be a much easier, fulfilling, and fun life. In other words, once you learn how to use dream incubation, you can create a dream life for yourself.

THE CREATIVE AND HEALING POWER OF DREAMS THROUGHOUT HISTORY

Asking dreams for guidance is not a new idea. Many ancient traditions viewed the dreamworld as sacred. Dreams and their inhabitants have been revered for their medicinal powers and guiding abilities, as the dreamworld contains knowledge that is applicable for healing and for accessing our own inner guidance. Indigenous cultures throughout Africa and on other continents believe that the dreamworld can be consulted for guidance and wisdom concerning all matters of life. All spiritual traditions believe that dreamers can ask questions about their relationships, vocation, spiritual queries, creative projects, and all matters related to physical and psychological healing. And sometimes, we need a little help boosting our level of enjoyment and fun in our daily lives; the dreamworld can help with that as well. Dream incubation is a simple concept—in its most basic application, it's learning how to ask your dream a question before you go to sleep in order to elicit a useful response in your dream.

There are well-documented traditions of dream incubation practices. Three thousand years ago in China, warrior kings used dream incubation for political concerns and to garner information about upcoming battles. Around 1500 A.D., dream incubation had become a generally practiced phenomena in Chinese culture. Then, it was common for people to ask questions like, "What do the ancestors want of me?" Or, "Will I pass my exam?" And, "What will the future bring for my family and community?" Furthermore, we see evidence from hunter-gatherer societies ranging from Scandinavian fisherman to Indigenous Americans where they asked their dreams for information on the best hunting spots and best sleeping and camping areas. They even sought information regarding who they should marry. The list goes on and on, and evidence of dream incubation is prevalent in almost every spiritual path. The Hindu text Chandogya Upanishad describes their dream incubation tradition. In Buddhism, it's found in the third yoga from Naropa. Islam's dream technique is called "Istakhara." And over the course of several conversations with African shamans, I was able to speak with them about how they sought information from the dreamworld. Dream incubation was, and had been, an integral part of their culture as long as they could remember. "Naturally, the Great Spirit knows everything and wants to help us in our lives," they assured me. There is even evidence of dream incubation happening in ancient Greece. Asclepius (the God of healing) is found at the center of their dream incubation rituals, which remained in practice for over a thousand years. A person would visit the Asclepeion temple, often suffering from a physical illness or a psychological problem, and then go through a series of rituals in preparation for one night in the holiest part of the temple. The individual would sleep on a couch and then have a healing dream. These dreams were then used by their doctor to provide a diagnosis, treatment plan, and healing path. At its core, Western medicine was born out of dreamwork.

In our contemporary culture, Freud and Jung are credited with recognizing the importance of our dreams for accessing healing information to aid in our psychological development. After a therapeutic session, Jung would often say, "Now let's see what your dream has to say about this." He'd consult the dreamworld about the ongoing therapeutic development of the patient.

We humans have always sought answers to our most urgent questions in life. I hope to show you that the best answers are contained within ourselves, and that all you need to do in order to retrieve them is learn and implement a dream incubation practice. In the chapters to follow, I'll help you understand how dreams can help you live your most authentic life.

CHAPTER 2

YOUR DREAM LIFE

Dream incubation emboldens you to take charge of your own life and turn it into a dream life. It can help you to tear down your own limiting beliefs, so that you can experience a richer and more joyous life. It provides you with tailor-made ways to deal with, for example, your health, your vocation, or finding a partner.

Jane is an elderly woman in her late 70s, with beautiful silver-gray hair, who had been raised in a religious tradition where it was more important to give to others than to take care of yourself. For several years she was confronted with the challenge of taking care of her increasingly immobile husband, who had dementia. Jane had been working around the clock the last several months as a wife, friend, nurse, caretaker, and cook, even getting out of bed in the middle of the night to help her husband go to the restroom. Like many partners in those situations, she struggled with how much energy she had to give, how much more she wanted to give, and how much she felt obligated to give. She had joined one of my dream groups. That week we asked the following question to the dream: "What is one limiting belief I have that hinders me the most?"

Jane had the following dream: "I am somewhere, and I meet some new people. I am asked to introduce myself, and I tell them my name, and I tell them that I am fixed, rigid in my life. Immediately, an inner voice yells out, 'No, that is not true!'"

The woman had the limiting belief that she had become fixed in her life, rigid in her care for her husband, and that she should be more flexible, more giving, and complain less. However, in being so accommodating, she was overextending herself and depleting her energy. Her own limiting belief made her feel that she needed to do more and more, and that she was stuck in her role. She was beginning to feel resentment and resistance. This dream was an inner confirmation that she was indeed working really hard and needed to rest and ask for more support in caring for her husband. By breaking down her limiting belief, the dream opened her up to a more joyful life.

Asking your dreams for help implies two very important aspects of this dream incubation technique. The first is that there is a direct relationship between you and dreaming. The second is that the answer is your own personal revelation. There is no need for outside help. Your own dream will guide you to find purpose and meaning.

PERSONAL RELATIONSHIP

Through dream incubation, you build and nurture your own relationship with the dreams. The elderly woman above asked her dream a question, and she got an answer from it. It is her relationship with the dream. The more you build and nurture this relationship, the more frequently you will experience the intuition of this inner voice. You will become better attuned to the suggestions and help it offers.

Everybody—every age, sex, ethnicity, and even if you have never remembered a dream in your life—has the ability to perform dream incubation. Everyone can at any moment start, develop, nurture, and grow that personal relationship. Dream incubation fosters personal growth and moves away from any form of co-dependence on other people, books, dogmas, organizations, or substances. It breaks any form of dependence that is in conflict with a genuine loving relationship with yourself, and therefore with your dreams. Dream incubation is your own direct relationship with dreaming, with no need of the interference of someone else.

PERSONAL REVELATION

The incubation dream is a personal revelation to you. It is your dream that reveals an answer to your question. One's own psyche is the birthplace of the dream that generates healing or creativity. Your own dream knows what is best for you, and this trumps any outside suggestion on how you should live your life. There is no exact formula on how to tease out your own blind spots and limiting beliefs, and there is no textbook that gives you the exact instructions for your specific life situation. However, the dream can do this for you. Once again, you don't need someone else, some book, or some organization to tell you how to live your life. As Jung says, the shoe that fits one person pinches another. Your dream will provide you with the right shoe.

Through dream incubation you are the authority on your own life, and you are in charge of co-creating your life. You can ask others to help you create a great question or puzzle on the dream answer; however, it is you who has the first and final say about what you ask, and how you work with the dream answer, and what you discover.

Carl Jung, Eastern religions like Buddhism and Hinduism, and other mystical traditions all stress the importance of one's own experience of life as the crucial factor for growth of consciousness. The Buddha asked his disciple Ananda once if he followed the Buddha because he liked him, believed in him, or if he understood the teachings and had realized them in himself. When Ananda said that he had understood his teachings and realized it for himself, the Buddha expressed his satisfaction. The Buddha said that no one should follow him or his ideas but should have the direct experience of them. To believe in something will not result in illumination. Dream incubation helps you do the same. The answer to your question has been hidden in your psyche; the dream simply reveals it.

CHAPTER 3

SPONTANEOUS GUIDING DREAMS

Dreams communicate with us even when we don't seek them out—these are spontaneous dreams, and we all experience them. Some of these spontaneous guiding dreams have contributed to the evolvement of the world and mankind. They have provided people with ground-breaking insights, wildly creative ideas, enchanting pieces of art, suggestions for social movements, breakthroughs in science—and they are even responsible for lives saved.

I want to take you on a journey through some dreams that have helped people in their lives. These are not incubation dreams that people sought out on purpose; they were spontaneous. There is a well-documented history of thousands of helpful spontaneous dreams—here are a few that showcase their tremendous impact.

We start our journey with a 22-year-old English man named Paul, who woke up one morning in dreary London. He had heard a catchy tune in his dream. He wondered whether it was an old song he had heard from his father, who liked old jazz music. This appeared not to be the case;

it was a novel song. Initially Paul used the working title "Scrambled Eggs," and later decided to call this song "Yesterday." This song by Paul McCartney and the Beatles has become the most played song of all time on the radio in the United States. This dream was a direct revelation or transmission of a piece of music that would enchant millions all over the world.

His friend and fellow band member John Lennon had noticed that he often would wake up with his best musical work in his mind. "The good stuff comes to you in the middle of the night, out of a creative space, and you have to get up and write it down."

All creative arts are known for their deep influence by the world of dream. Numerous musicians have had their music come to them in their dreams. Later on, you will learn how you can increase your own openness to and revelations of artistic inspiration.

Another dream-inspired story that changed the course of a man and his country is that of Gandhi. This thin lawyer, dressed in a simple and humble cloth, took on a monumental task of peacefully freeing his people from the 300-year oppression by a different nation. In 1919 a law was passed in India curtailing civil liberties of Indians. Gandhi argued in court against it yet was unsuccessful.

In the night after the ruling of the court, Gandhi reported, "The idea came to me, last night in a dream that we should call upon the country to observe a general hartal [hunger strike]."[1] He set himself to the task of implementing this dream suggestion, and on April 6 the whole nation of India observed a day of fasting. This dream started the journey of nonviolent resistance, and many more hunger strikes, finally resulting in a social movement that would overthrow the English rulership of India in 1947.

Now I would like to share another artistic development that is based on the suggestions of dream beings. William lived in the 18th and 19th centuries in England and became a poet, painter, and printmaker. From an early age, he had intense dreams, and he learned to pay attention to them. Besides having a dream being come to him that gave him images to paint, William was also visited by his deceased brother in the dream who told him how to improve his engraving technique, which worked. These days William—William Blake—is probably most known for his poetry.

What is interesting in the William Blake dream reports is that he is being visited by a dream being that is a help to him, and he is also visited by his deceased brother. This dream being is what we in the next chapter will encounter again: a daimon, or what the Romans would call a genius. This dream being, or daimon, is an example of what we'll encounter again in the next chapter. The Romans called daimons "geniuses," or helping dream figures that would assist in one's life.

It is a commonly reported phenomena to be visited by deceased loved ones, and these belong to the most powerful and intense dreams people often have. These visitation dreams often leave a deep impact and can be very healing or instructive.

Dream inspiration comes not only to the artistic field but also to the hard sciences. In 1936 the Jewish–German researcher Otto Loewi stretched out his hands to receive the Nobel prize for medicine. Again, the world of dream had made a suggestion, and Otto had felt its importance. On the night before Easter, 16 years earlier, Otto describes: "I awoke, turned on the light and jotted down a few notes on a tiny slip of thin paper. Then I fell asleep again. It occurred to me at six o'clock in the morning that during the night I had written down something important, but I was unable to decipher the scrawl. The next night, at three o'clock, the idea returned. It was the design of an experiment to determine whether the hypothesis of chemical transmission that I had uttered 17 years ago was correct. I got up immediately, went to the laboratory, and performed a simple experiment on a frog heart according to the nocturnal design."[2]

Loewi's dream thus led to the discovery that the primary language of nerve cell communication is chemical and not electrical. The dream comes up with a groundbreaking suggestion that pushes the world of medicine to a new frontier. It was such a revolutionary idea that it got awarded with a Nobel prize.

Here is an example of one of the great Western dream doctors of the last century, Carl Jung, who said: "Dreams have influenced all the important changes in my life and theories." At the end of his life, when he was already well into his 80s, Jung was asked to write a general introduction book to his theories. Jung initially listened politely to the idea of the publication and declined firmly. However, he soon after that had the following dream. "He dreamed that, instead of sitting in his study and talking to the great doctors and psychiatrists who used to call on him from all over the world, he was standing in a public place and addressing a multitude of people who were listening to him with rapt attention and understanding what he said."[3]

When the stubborn publisher tried to persuade Jung, two weeks later, again of this idea of a book for the general public, Jung agreed to it, and this is how we got Jung's book *Man and His Symbols*. This book was also the first book that I read by Jung; I was tremendously impressed, and it opened the world of dream to me. I am very grateful for the work Jung did, as he created a door through which I could engage with the world of dream.

All religious traditions speak of spontaneous dreams, and all of these traditions either see the dream as a medium through which the Divine communicates or in which people can get spiritual teachings.

Both in the Bible and in the Quran, we find the story of the dreamer and dream interpreter Joseph when he is in prison and he interprets the dreams of his fellow inmates, or when he interprets the dream of the pharaoh. Joseph works with dreams pertaining to the future, so-called "precognitive dreams," or prophetic dreams. These prophetic dreams are common dreams in cultures around the world.

Yet spontaneous guiding dreams don't happen only to the exceptional genius or to well-known people. Spontaneous dreams happen to everybody, and some people have more of a tendency to listen to their dreams and pick up on some of these helpful suggestions than other people. Yet there are some dreams that have been standing out. Here is one I enjoyed hearing from a participant in one of my dream workshops in Marrakesh. This man tells us the following spontaneous life-saving dream.

"During my studies as a medical student in Bloemfontein, my brother and I had an arrangement to fetch the campus newspaper from the printers in our hometown, Potchefstroom. It was 600 km roundtrip, and few other people had the stomach for it. We did it for the money. We also got to see our parents and filled up our empty food boxes with rusks and food from Mom's pantry. On one particular trip, we could only leave Bloemfontein at midnight. My brother and I both sang in the men's residence choir, which had a performance that night. The deal was that he would drive to Potchefstroom while I slept, and then I would drive back to Bloemfontein, being well rested. My roommate at the time, Stephen, was not impressed with our plan and warned me a few times that he thought it was a bad and dangerous idea. But we knew the road well, and being headstrong, pushed ahead with our plan. My brother got us to Potchefstroom at 3 A.M., and we loaded our Toyota Corolla with the few thousand copies of the IRAWA newspaper. I bought a can of Red Bull and set off for Bloemfontein with my brother sleeping next to me. About 100 km into the return journey, I fell asleep behind the steering wheel. It happened quite promptly and without warning. As I fell asleep, I had a dream. In my dream I was at a typical campus residence house party. There were lots of people, music, and beer. I walked into the house and through the front door and found myself staring down a long corridor. The music was intense, and this was the core of the party. Pushing and shoving my way through the crowd, I walked to the other end of the corridor where I found my roommate Stephen waiting for me. He was furious. He walked right up to me, grabbed my shirt in front of my chest, and punched me in the face while shouting: 'I told you, you shouldn't fucking drive!' As the punch landed on my face, I woke up behind the steering wheel with the first set of wheels slipping off the tarmac and onto the gravel indicating the shoulder of the road. I stopped the car, got out, and acknowledged the miracle and lifesaving dream I had. My brother and I took turns to drive the next 200 km and stayed awake with each other. On arrival at my residence at sunrise, I told Stephen of the dream and how it saved my life. He just smiled and said: 'Come, let's go have breakfast.'"

Several years ago, I had a spontaneous dream that I took as a suggestion to build the Jung Society of Utah and Jung Platform. That was a vocational dream.

These spontaneous guiding dreams have benefited the recipients of the dream in their life and in some cases as a consequence millions of people around the world.

However, we don't have to wait for a spontaneous dream to appear. We don't need to wait until the dream reaches out to us. Rather, we can build a relationship with the dream. We can reach out and ask this wise and creative spirit for a helpful dream using the ancient method of dream incubation. But before we dive in and learn more about dream incubation, let's take a deeper look at the innate desire that the dream has to help us.

CHAPTER 4

THE DREAM IS INTERESTED IN HELPING US

The dream is interested in helping us. We have seen in the previous chapter that the dream can spontaneously provide enchanting pieces of music and art, breakthrough developments in science, help start a social movement, and even save lives.

However, we don't need to wait till the dream comes spontaneously with support—we can proactively ask the dream to help us with whatever we need, whether the issue is romantic, professional, financial, or health related.

This thought that there is help out there is old. In almost all the wisdom traditions, we find references to this encouraging idea. We all know the biblical saying in Matthew: "Ask and it will be given to you; seek and you will find; knock and the door will be opened to you." Several sentences later this is confirmed and emphasized with "your Father in heaven gives good gifts to those who ask him."[1]

In the holy book of Islam, the Quran, Allah says: "Call on me; I will respond to you."[2] Allah encourages a proactive reaching out, which is considered an act of worship. Asking Allah to respond through a dream is a spiritual practice of being in touch with the great and merciful creator of the universe.

The mystical 13th-century Sufi poet Rumi describes the relationship between man and the Divine as follows:

> *There is no lover seeking union,*
>
> *Without the beloved searching for him, too.*
>
> *A thirsty person cries for fresh water,*
>
> *While water is crying: "who wants to drink me."*

Rumi is indicating that the relationship between man and the Divine is a love affair, both searching for each other. Our thirst for the Divine is only answered by the Divine's cry of being taken in.

In my travels to Africa to learn about Indigenous healing methods, I trained with several different African shamans. They taught me that in their tradition, the first line of support in the world of dream is the ancestors. By "ancestors" they usually mean personal blood ancestors, but they can also mean anyone who has passed on. Not infrequently it also refers to those spirits who are commonly known as spirit guides, guardian angels, or daimons. In these African traditions that I encountered, you are encouraged to nurture the relationship to the ancestors on a daily basis, and to inform them when you have a challenge and need help. It is thought that the ancestors will help proactively, yet that their full help and support can become fully active only if you ask them.

This is the overall idea in all of these spiritual and religious traditions. There is help out there, and it works spontaneously, yet when we ask specifically for what we need, it can and will give us more guidance.

Another tradition that I want to reference is from current-day psychology. One of Carl Jung's most gifted pupils was Marie-Louise von Franz. She states that "the actual processes of individuation, the conscious coming-to-terms with one's own inner center or Self, generally begins with a wounding of the personality." The ego reaches an impasse of one sort or another and has to turn for help to the Self. She describes the Jungian Self as the "psychic center that organizes the life path and growth," and it is the "inventor of the dreams."[3] In classical Jungian thought, then, the Self is the regulating, directing center that sends dreams to help.

Another practice that shows experientially that there is a larger awareness present in or behind the dream is lucid dreaming. Robert Waggoner is one of the most interesting Western lucid dreamers currently alive. He developed great questions to ask in the dream state, and through a series of experiences and growing his consciousness-expanding journey, he started to notice that there was a "larger awareness" behind the dream that was helping him on his lucid quest. Waggoner said that this "larger awareness" behind the dream "is interested in educating and instructing."

All of these traditions point out that there is a Mystery that responds positively to being asked a question. It appears that this Mystery's full help can only be released when it is proactively engaged, and when it is being asked for help with specific areas of your life.

I decided to ask the dream a question about this topic before I went to sleep. I created the following question: "Dream, what message would you want to share with readers about asking you for help?"

This is the Dream response: "There is a new female manager of the company, she is really great and effective. I got the feeling that she is very kind and extremely competent. She is an excellent manager; she is always willing to help, and will also give you trust and time to figure it out on your own, no matter how long that took. Both options are totally fine for her."

To me this dream suggests that the Mystery is interested in helping, enjoys it, and is extremely competent in doing so. Yet there is also free will. It seems that the Mystery will give people total freedom to choose, and appears nonjudgmental to their choice. That is likely why these spiritual traditions emphasize that one needs to ask to experience the full help from the Mystery.

However, what about that time when my mother was really ill and I prayed and she still died, or when I asked for help in my business, and it still did not flourish? Or, if I can ask and it will be given, then please deliver a Ferrari to my house this afternoon. We tried, and we don't see the results. We know that indeed not every request is fulfilled. Are these passages in the Bible or Quran that God or Allah answers your questions just feel-good statements?

The dream is indeed not the genie in Aladdin, who resides in the magical oil lamp and fulfills any request the person has. In Chapter 8, "What Shall I Ask My Dream Tonight?," I explore in detail which questions work and which usually won't lead to the answer a person wants. Even if the dream is not a wish-fulfilling genie, it is interested in helping you with your life path. Requests that don't support your life path often generate little support. Fulfilling any wish that you have might not be conducive for you and your path. The Dalai Lama once said: "Remember that sometimes not getting what you want is a wonderful stroke of luck."

No fulfillment of your request might also be an answer. The basic idea is that the dream is interested in helping you with living your life, finding your life path, and even transforming it into a joyous life, where possible.

PERSONAL GUIDES

There is more help available besides that of the Mystery. Traditionally, many cultures believe that there are specific helpers who live in the world of dream who are allocated to assist us on our life journey. This is one of the most widespread belief systems around the world. In the Greek tradition this figure is called the "daimon," and in Roman times the "genius." This daimon/genius is different from the Mystery itself; it is a figure that stands between man and the Mystery. This daimon should not be mixed up with the Christian idea of the demon. The demon is a negative figure, whereas the daimon or genius is a personal guide and helper. There are several ways we can connect with this figure, and the most popular route is through dreams.

THE DAIMON: GUIDE, TALENT, AND TASKMASTER

The *daimon* is the Greek word for that figure that is also referred to as a guardian angel, genius, muse, the resident spirit of the soul, and in some African traditions, the Divine Twin.[4]

The daimon is a guide who reminds us of our callings. It is our sense of having a talent. It is also felt as a forceful taskmaster. When we are connected to our daimon, we often have a sense of being in the flow—fulfilled and never bored. Other times, however, it feels like a struggle.

The Roman name for the daimon is the "genius," and comes from the North African word *geni*, which means "the gifted spirit who was already there." It is considered that this gifted spirit is separate from you and joins you in this lifetime. Therefore, you are not a genius, you have a genius. That is an important distinction, and more about that later.

The Greek word *Eudaimonia*, which is often translated as "happiness" or "flourishing," means that you and your daimon are together. In this old Greek tradition, it is seen as the goal of life to be with your daimon, so that the daimon may live through you and distribute its gifts to the world.

There are many ways to nurture the relationship with the daimon. The prime way to meet the daimon is in your dreams, to nurture the relationship through following your dreams, and by engaging in dream incubation. The daimon wants to help us, but unlike the Mystery, it will sometimes force that help upon us.

The good news is that everybody—not just people we deem exceptional—is allocated a daimon, or has a genius. These days, we usually reserve the name "genius" for incredibly intelligent people with high IQs. These people just have a daimon with strong intellectual capabilities. Yet every person has a genius, no matter their social class, gender, race, religion, or age.

Even better news, we are actually allocated several daimons. Some stay for a lifetime, while others come in and out during our life's journey.

There is the tendency to think that the daimon or genius relates to an exceptional talent, yet that is not who it is. The daimon or genius is a talent that can come in many forms: some small, some big. Some want a public stage; others seek a role in their immediate environment. All are equally valuable.

Being connected to one's genius means expressing your talent; sometimes this turns into a job or career, and other times it is something that people have to offer: friendship, beautifying a home, cooking a meal, the ability to listen, being funny. It can also manifest as a hobby, such as football, painting, or weaving. Sometimes the genius is a peculiarity, such as following the weather reports around the world with no practical application for it whatsoever.

When a person connects to their genius, then they become unique and authentic. They grow out of the norm and are no longer someone who mindlessly goes through the motions of life.

When the genius lives through us, then we will display a specific style and unique quality. You can see it in athletes or artists who have a signature to their activity that is uniquely theirs. It is not only that they play a sport or make art, but how they do it.[5]

This all sounds fun, exciting, and worthwhile. So why isn't everybody hanging out with his or her daimon all the time then?

Jung says, "The man, therefore, who, driven by his daimon, steps beyond the limits of the intermediary stage, truly enters the untrodden, untreadable regions. Where there are no charted ways and no shelter spreads a protecting roof over his head. There are no precepts to guide him when he encounters an unforeseen situation for example, a conflict of duties."[6]

Following your daimon also means that you could have to sometimes take a rather big risk, such as leaving a job, home, or relationship. You will be venturing into the unknown, and the truly unknown is discomforting. The daimon can also be a ruthless taskmaster, which makes it difficult to follow at times.

It takes courage to listen to the daimon's suggestions and directions, and to be truly creative and authentic. However, nothing has as much lasting effect on one's sense of fulfillment, happiness, and genuine self-worth as following the daimon. One is then truly living a dream life. Let's take a look at how the daimon reminds us of our calling and keeps us on our life path.

THE DAIMON AS GUIDE

Ancient Greeks believed that individuals were attached at birth to a daimon who determined, wholly or in part, their destiny.[7] The daimon influences your destiny, as the daimon will always seek the most fertile ground for you to live out your talents. The daimon will guide you into those life experiences where you are called to dig into yourself and bring out your talent.

The unique and brilliant psychologist James Hillman sums it up very well: "A personal daimon is an accompanying guide who remembers your calling . . . the daimon motivates. It protects. It invents and persists with stubborn fidelity. It resists compromising reasonableness and often forces deviance and oddity upon its keeper, and especially when it is neglected or opposed."[8]

In the role of guide, the daimon keeps calling us. We can see this clearly in the realm of dreams: the daimon will show up and bring those spontaneous helpful dreams that urge us to move in a certain direction.

As an accompanying guide, your daimon remembers your calling. Your daimon also appears to be almost exclusively interested in helping you fulfill your calling. That is why when asking for help, requests that are associated with your calling are often willingly answered. Those requests that might not be linked to your calling, or that might even stand between you and living out your daimon in this world, might not be fulfilled. This is a further explanation as to why the dream will not necessarily provide you with that Ferrari but will step forward to give you clues that are necessary for your calling.

DAIMON AS TALENT

The Roman version of the daimon is the genius, and in the word *genius* we see how it refers to someone's talent. The genius is a talent, an aptitude, a way of seeing and being in the world.

Remember that a person is not a genius; a person has a genius. In our day and age, people often tend to think about the personality as a single figure. This "I" thinks it operates alone, and appropriates all feelings, intuitions, thoughts, insights into itself. But if we implement the way of daimonic thinking, we understand that we are actually just the front man in a larger enterprise. We are a conglomerate of figures that makes up one person. To think this way helps us not to confuse ourselves with our talent, because when we do this, it often leads to some form of arrogance, or on the other hand, a lack of self-worth. The gift of the daimon is not to be exploited; we should be in service to it and deliver it to the world.

We can learn to have a relationship to the daimon, and practice embodying it in this life. When we do that, we can express our talent, an action that generates genuine self-worth and fulfillment. The daimon calls us to partici-pate in the creation of the world. When we participate the daimon is expressed, and the world experiences that as a gift, and we live a dream life.

The daimon is already present and cannot be made.

This provides a different psychological model of thinking about the world and about our own devel-opment. Instead of thinking we start a project empty handed, we know that we already have our daimon. We all have an inborn talent that wants to come out, and we have to become aware of it and start relating to it. Only when we learn how to embody the daimon can it express itself. For example, a soccer player is not developing his talent; he is learning how his soccer daimon can best inhabit him. When the daimon inhabits him well, he will say that he is in the flow. He and his daimon are seen together—Eudaimonia.

The daimon is interested in our lives and is calling us to awaken to its assistance and desire to participate in this world. It communicates in different ways to foster a rela-tionship with us, yet the prime arena is in the world of dream. We can use dream incubation to figure out who our daimon is, what it wants, and how we can thank it for its ongoing participation in our lives.

THE DAIMON AS TASKMASTER

Jung remarks, "The daimon of creativity has ruthlessly had its way with me." The daimon made Jung work at home, or in his tower in Bollingen, while others were hav-ing fun with friends and family. The daimon will not let someone slumber and rest when a creative project needs to be finished. In those cases, you will have a chronic nagging feeling that you need to work, and it won't go away until you give yourself over to the task at hand. You might even have a feeling that the world is conspiring against you.

James Hillman adds, "A personal daimon . . . resists compromising reasonableness and often forces deviance and oddity upon its keeper and especially when it is neglected or opposed."⁹ The daimon might then show up in nightmares. Therefore, Jung reports that he would write and labor, and miss out on some of the pleasantries of human life. The daimon demanded ruthlessly that he would go his own way and leave friendships in favor of his creative contribution.

The experience of the daimon is not some lofty transcendental experience; that only happens in some rare incidences. The daimon is present all the time, and we just need to learn to notice its presence. Jung says the daimon is our "instincts"; it "comes to us from within, as a compulsion or will or command." Jung goes on to say that our compulsion or will or command has given "more or less . . . from time immemorial—the name of a personal daimon."¹⁰

This happens to all of us. We just have to listen to what our instincts tell us, pay attention to what our fascinations are, what we fantasize about, what strikes us, what it is that we see in the world, where our eyes are drawn to, what we love and fear. Our feelings and thoughts are often the way that the daimon communicates with us.

This is how Steve Jobs describes the experience of the importance and experience of the daimon in everyday life: "Your time is limited, so don't waste it living someone else's life. Don't be trapped by dogma, which is living with the results of other people's thinking. Don't let the noise of other's opinions drown out your own inner voice. And most important, have the courage to follow your heart and intuition. They somehow already know what you truly want to become. Everything else is secondary."[11]

The Irish poet William Butler Yeats refers to the task-master aspect of the daimon in his book *Mythologies*: "I think it was Heraclitus who said: the Daimon is our destiny. When I think of life as a struggle with the Daimon who would ever set us to the hardest work among those not impossible, I understand why there is a deep enmity between a man and his destiny, and why a man loves nothing but his destiny. . . ."[12]

The first step is to figure out who your daimon is, and the second step is to learn to live with that daimon. The daimon is like a challenging coach who stretches our capacity and urges us to give a little bit more than what we think we are capable of.

HOW TO SPOT A DAIMON IN THE DREAM

There are many different ways that the daimon can present itself to you in your dream. It can show up in any form it likes, yet they are commonly seen as an old wise man or woman, a magician, a dwarf, an elf, a fairy, a friendly or stern helpful figure, a coach, a guru, one's therapist, an animal (especially when they can speak), or as an alien. These days, the daimon might also show up as a sports hero or movie star. This is a limited list of an exhaustive variation of forms they can take on.

Not all dream figures are daimons, yet the figures that Jung would call the "mana" personalities—figures that exude some form of authority or power—are believed to fall into this realm.

THE DREAM IS INTERESTED IN HELPING US

Religions like Christianity and Islam have made the bold and encouraging statement that the Mystery is interested in helping humans on their path through life. One of the most common mythologies around the world states that there is also a helper allocated to each one of us at birth: a daimon, genius, or spirit guide, who will remind us of our calling, assist us in delivering its gifts, and keep us on task. We are truly not alone.

The helper will communicate to us through dreams— it will spontaneously come up with solutions, but its full help can be bestowed on us when we proactively reach out, engage with it, and ask for assistance. You can ask this helping force all kinds of dream incubation questions, including if it has a message for you, how you can thank it for its help, or what its current and most pressing interest for you is. In Chapter 6 we will explore more dream incubation questions you can ask your daimon, and examples of building and nurturing this relationship with the helping force.

But before we do that, let's explore the fascinating and fundamental ways that dream incubators from cultures around the globe engaged in the process.

CHAPTER 5

CONNECTING TO OUR FELLOW DREAM INCUBATORS

I'm thrilled, excited, and there are butterflies in my stomach. I am walking in the invisible footsteps of thousands and thousands of ill people, who have come to this dream healing temple of Asclepius in Epidaurus, Greece. The place exudes aliveness and has a welcoming atmosphere. The beauty of the environment is soothing, and the expectation of a special encounter is heightened.

With every step I feel the vibrant connection to a mainstream tradition that lasted for a thousand years, in which people consulted the dream for healing. The reports are full of people healing from all kinds of illnesses, ranging from blindness, infertility, being paralyzed, and body pains to emotional and psychological problems. The god Asclepius would also prescribe lifestyle changes, diet, exercise, and creative expressions. The many votives speak to the cures and healings that took place at these temples.

This is one of the 320 temples dedicated to the healing god Asclepius. These temples dedicated to healing through dreams did flourish at the same time that the world witnessed in Greece the birth of democracy, tragedy and plays, architectonical wonders, art, and flourishing philosophy. Some of the most influential and creative people in Western history, such as Plato and Socrates, walked around here and were intimately interconnected with this healing tradition. Plato was ill the day before Socrates was executed. Socrates told Plato to sleep at the temple of Asclepius, and when he would wake up cured, that he should sacrifice a cock to Asclepius.

For me it was a sacred pilgrimage to go to Epidaurus and explore how the old Greeks and Romans did dream incubation. In the old days, people who sought healing and guidance would go on a pilgrimage, often traveling for days to come to this temple where there were 160 rooms to stay. The supplicants would then go through a process of preparation and rituals till they would be ready to spend the night in the special dream room, the abaton in the temple, to encounter the healing god Asclepius. The next day, this experience would be followed up with working on their dream with the temple therapist. These four phases of the process—the pilgrimage, the preparations, the healing night, and the work on the dream—were deeply effective.

In this chapter we will explore cultures and traditions in which people engaged in dream incubation. We will connect with those who share our interest in proactively connecting with the dream for guidance and healing. These are people like Plato and Socrates, biblical figures like King Solomon and Daniel, any shaman that lives or has ever lived, and the people within spiritual traditions—such as Istakhara in Islam and the Upanishad in Hinduism—that encourage consulting the Divine through dreams. Dream incubation was a common practice for many ancient cultures: the Greeks and Romans consulted Asclepius, and the Chinese dream culture that flourished in the 16th and 17th centuries. We will also explore what these people did to trigger the most optimal dream response, so that we can mimic their patterns of success. And that is where we start.

THE SUCCESSFUL ASCLEPEION DREAM INCUBATION PROCESS

One of the more elaborate and well-documented dream incubation traditions is the Asclepeion tradition that I explored on my journey to Greece and Turkey. When I meandered over these large compounds, the remains and ruins gave a sense of the majesty and grandeur of these healing places. The aesthetic interplay between the warm beauty of the temples and the gorgeous natural environment was inviting, and that in itself seemed to make me feel energized. I was struck by the sheer size of the temple complexes in Epidaurus, Kos, and Pergamon. The complexes are spacious and surrounded by hills, with large temples, sacred pools and fountains, and beautiful pine trees. There are overnight rooms to stay for hundreds of people, special dream incubation rooms, underground tunnels, and a theater.

The theater in Epidaurus holds 14,000 people, and each guest was able to hear the play due to the exquisite acoustics. These were the heydays of the Greek plays and tragedies that are still known to us. In that time, culture and creativity flourished, the Greeks had a living relationship to their gods, and they turned to the dream to connect to guiding forces.

It is thrilling to stand eye to eye with a culture that took dream incubation very seriously, that built these exquisite temples in magnificent locations, had an elaborate process for healing and incubation, and spectacular results due to it.

There were thousands of votives remaining from people who were healed due to this process. With that, let us take a look at the process of successful dream incubation.

THE DREAM INCUBATION PROCESS IS A RITUAL

In a way, we could say that the whole dream incubation procedure is a ritual. We are inviting the world of dream to participate in our daily lives and grind the boundaries of this reality so that there is a constant merging of the dreamworld with us. Any activity can be a ritual if we define it in this way—if it is done with the intention to invite in the world of dream. In the same way, an activity cannot be a ritual if the world of dream is not present. If a ritual has become stale, then the world of dream wasn't there. The aliveness of the activity is a reflection of the participation of the world of dream.

Participating in the right rituals is essential, as that will get you in the right frequency to receive an answer to your question.

FOUR PHASES OF THE ASCLEPEION DREAM INCUBATION PROCESS

For ease I have divided the Asclepeion dream incubation process into four phases: the pilgrimage toward the healing temple, the preparations and rituals, the night in the temple, and the day after to work on the dream with a therapist.

The first phase: the pilgrimage is in a literal way the road to the temple. It is a journey undertaken out of loss or desire, with the aim to connect with the wisdom and healing powers of the dream.

The pilgrimage is often to a place of deep significance. In this Greek tradition, one would go to the temple. In other traditions, one would undertake a journey to a sacred cave, isolated place in the desert, mountaintop, or any other special place where one then would sleep, dream, and engage with the world of dream and its inhabitants.

A pilgrimage is both a journey to an external place and an internal spiritual journey. Through journeying to the external temple, we open up to the world of dream and can experience its presence.

The pilgrimage is a physical manifestation of the intention to find a cure or answer, and the effort one is willing to put into it. While walking for days to the sacred temple, one would be filled with expectations, the intent and will to get better, a focus on one's healing journey, and the belief that this would be helpful. These facets are part of the functioning ingredients of a ritual.

Also note that Robert Waggoner identified these five principles: intent, will, focus, beliefs, and expectation as the dream-reality-creating principles. According to Waggoner's experiments, these five elements, together with mystery factor X, are the principles that build up the dream reality. The dreamworld responds in a different way to these reality-creating principles, yet these principles also contribute to the creation of this reality we live in during the day. I believe these principles are also part of the working ingredients in the placebo.

These principles get stronger by undertaking a pilgrimage, and the stronger they are, the stronger the dream response. The pilgrimage helps a person to be in the right frequency for the dreamworld to flow in and provide healing, wisdom, and guidance.

Putting conscious effort and attentiveness into the pilgrimage increases its value and efficacy. In our times we could consider going to a special place to dream or selecting a date in the future to do the dream incubation and consider the time until then as the pilgrimage. On your pilgrimage you can be attentive to your own musings, your recent dreams, surprises along the way, synchronicities, and by repeating your desire to find healing or a creative response.

Rituals are personalized activities to relate and invite to the world of dream, so any other form you come up with that creates a sense of pilgrimage is welcome.

PREPARATIONS AND RITUALS AT THE TEMPLE

After the journey, the pilgrims would experience the joyous moment of arriving at the temple complex. The location of these temples is carefully chosen, in the middle of a valley surrounded by hills and green trees, or on the top of a hill with a view of the sparkling blue Mediterranean Sea. The white marble temples would inspire a sense of awe. One was surrounded by the therapists at the temple, who would support the process, and other supplicants, who were on the shared journey to receive healing. This would warm one's soul in those places where it had become colder due to the pain, fear, and isolation of being ill.

At the temple the supplicant would start with the preparations and rituals for the healing night. The preparations and rituals usually lasted for several days, and one would wait for a sign in a dream or in day-to-day life that would indicate that they were ready to undertake the healing night: the night in which they would sleep in the dream room and encounter Asclepius.

Let us put you in the seat of the supplicant so that you may better understand the sacred process. In the days before the healing night, you would spend time with the therapists. They would remind you that the god Asclepius is willing to help, and your faith would increase by seeing the many votives given by all of those people who experienced healing at the temple. The therapists would also check your overall health and make lifestyle and ritual recommendations.

Throughout the day you would engage in rituals, cleansing, and purification through sitting in a sacred pool, leaning backward, and breathing into your stomach so you would feel the sun on your skin and the water supporting and caressing your body while your eyes feasted on the beautiful nature around you. You would sit there with other people, coming from different parts of the country with the same aim as you. When you sat with them in the sacred pool, you would feel the human warmth that comes from this shared undertaking, this shared suffering and desire to heal.

People would be making music, and you could join in. Throughout the day you would engage in spontaneous prayers, and you would make sacrifices and offerings to Asclepius.

You would preferably be wearing light clothing. For some people, there would be special meals; other people might be guided to fast. You would also be in the presence of people who had already experienced the healing night, and to be with people who have had a positive experience increases your hope.

All of these experiences and rituals would prepare you for a successful dream incubation night. You would be in the right emotional state to encounter the god of medicine and healing, Asclepius, in your dream.

The Dream Night: At nightfall, you would feel the tension of participating in the Dream Night. You would have worked up to this moment for days, and now the night had arrived. Questions would run through your mind: Would Asclepius also reveal himself to me? Would the cure happen? Moments of doubt and uncertainty are part of the process.

You would enter the special dream incubation room in the temple, the abaton, and find your space on the couch. You could hear singing from the other parts of the temple, while the candles burned, and harmless snakes would occasionally slither by. During the night, in the sleep state, or in one of those fertile states between dreaming and waking, one would have an encounter with Asclepius. This encounter could take on different forms: sometimes one would meet Asclepius in his traditional form depicted in the temple or statues. Other times Asclepius would shape-shift into an animal or another figure. There are reports of people having whole dialogues with Asclepius. In any case, the night experience would result in a cure, diagnosis, prescription, or a suggestion on how to be with one's problem.

The next day, you would meet with the therapist to work on your dream. You would need to follow up with some specific activities on the dream. You would also be encouraged to display some sense of gratitude for the received dream—an important yet underperformed part of dream healing and dreamwork in general.

We can learn from this elaborate Asclepeion practice of dream incubation and model our own engagement with the healing and guiding powers in the world of dream on it.

CONNECTING TO FELLOW DREAM INCUBATORS

It was a life-transforming experience for me to be at the Asclepeion temple in Epidaurus and to experience the joy and warmth of connecting with the culture that had a profound respect for the dream and its healing power. This culture had built a relationship with the dream that was more elaborate than mine, yet in ways it was similar to what I had done.

In this moment, you and I also connect in our interest and exploration of the guiding and healing power of dreams. We also connect back in time with the old Greek and Roman man and woman who visited the temple of Asclepius. We connect with all of those people and traditions throughout history who consulted the dream for healing and guidance. It is profound to sense this connection. We connect with the known and many unknown people in our current time who practice dream incubation.

Let's explore who some of our fellow dream incubation practitioners are:

The first recorded dream incubation practice is in *The Epic of Gilgamesh*, an epic poem from around 2500 B.C. Gilgamesh asked the mountain for a dream on his journey to the forest. On the third day, they drew near Lebanon. They dug a well facing Shamash (the setting sun). Gilgamesh climbed up a mountain peak, made a libation of flour, and said: "Mountain, bring me a dream, a favorable message from Shamash."

In this first dream incubation report, we see similar features to what we found in the Asclepeion process. Gilgamesh sleeps in a special place, engages in a ritual, and asks for the dream.

Another group of people with whom we share our fascination for helpful dreams are the Egyptians. A papyrus role was found in Egypt dating from the year 2000 B.C. The old Egyptians believed that dreams contained divine communication. The procedure described in one papyrus roll is as follows: "The person requiring communication would write their request on a piece of linen, along with the name of the deity being called upon. The cloth would then be rolled up and used as a lamp wick. As the lamp burned, a prayer would be said and the dreamer would then lie down to sleep in the hope (and expectation) of receiving a dream."[1]

DREAMING INCUBATION IN ISLAM: ISTAKHARA

Several years ago, I was in South Africa giving a series of lectures and workshops on dreams. Being and dreaming in South Africa is always exciting for me, as I was born there. I met up with a friend in Johannesburg who told me a dream incubation story about her uncle who lives in India. Years ago, when this uncle was about to enter into an arranged marriage, he made sure to consult with the dream whether this marriage was going to be beneficial for him. This man was a devout Muslim, and in the Islamic tradition one can engage in "Istakhara," a form of dream incubation. The uncle did two special evening prayers, and asked Allah for guidance on one of the biggest decisions he would make in his life. Would it be beneficial for him to enter into this marriage? In the dream that followed, the uncle saw the traditional wedding sweets that are often handed out to guests. He took that as a favorable indication, and he married the woman. Now 25 years later the uncle reports that this marriage has indeed been sweet to him.

Istakhara comes from the root word *khayr*, which means "beneficence." Istakhara means to ask Allah to guide one to the right thing concerning any affair in one's life. One can do this in waking time and wait for a response, or through asking the dream a question. It is especially common to do Istakhara for guidance on marriage, business, or political affairs.

Just as with the dream incubation process of Asclepius, in this tradition it is also encouraged to go and dream in a spiritual place such as a cave, temple, or grave of a spiritual person. The prescribed Istakhara ritual is to do two special prayers, in addition to the regular five daily prayers. As part of the prayer, one meditates on the concern one brings in. One is free to add any other ritual to it as well.

It is very interesting that this tradition also has developed ways to interpret the dream response. If one dreams about white or green colors, in any form, then that would be favorable. If one receives images of peace, benevolence, beauty, or positive spiritual figures, then that would naturally also be a positive sign.

In his book *The Dream in Islam*, Iain Edgar reports that one businessman, the son of a former leader of an Islamic country, wonders whether he should invest in a business opportunity. After doing Istakhara, he dreams of a large white cake that is cut into pieces. He has a happy feeling in the dream. As white is an advantageous color, he invests, and later on when the money is returned on his investment, it is much more than expected.[2]

If one were to dream about the colors red, black, or yellow, or see destructive images, the response would be considered negative.

This way of working with the dream response, based on favorable and unfavorable images, is in line with my suggestions in Chapter 12 on how to work with a dream.

Dream incubation is found in almost any spiritual, religious, or Indigenous tradition. Even the "Dalai Lama has found it useful to instruct initiates in dream incubation practices involving special prayers, sleep postures and kusha grass (to be put under one's mattress and pillows as agents of purification)."[3]

I am familiar with some of the African Indigenous traditions, and likely because I was born in South Africa, I have an innate connection with the African spiritual customs. Less than a decade ago, dreams started to lead me to connect with the South African *sangoma*—healers who work with ancestral spirits—and diviners. Once, I woke up from a dream the morning that I went to a conference at my alma mater, Pacifica Graduate Institute. In the dream, the plane I was on landed in Johannesburg, South Africa. Touching the ground with the plane generated a marvelous feeling of coming home, and in the dream, I was deeply emotional and touched. There was a sense of ecstatic joy of arriving back in South Africa. I went to the conference filled with longing for my home. At the conference, there happened to be a South African medical doctor and sangoma talking about the South African shamanic paradigm and dreams. We connected and became friends—this was my first connection to a sangoma. As a result of this encounter, I regularly visited with the shamans in and from South Africa and with the West African elder and shaman diviner Malidoma Somé. I have been initiated as a shamanic diviner and explored in depth the way that these traditions consult with the world of dream and its inhabitants. Any of the African shamans I encountered found it most natural to proactively consult the dream and its inhabitants for help, guidance, and healing.

The overall worldview in these African Indigenous cultures that I encountered had the following same basic underpinnings of any Indigenous shamanic culture. Those core beliefs are the notion of there being another world, co-existing with this world, inhabited with ancestors, spirits, and other beings, with whom one can have a relationship. The world of dream is part of that other world.

A MIDSUMMER NIGHT IN SCANDINAVIA

If we move to the bright and long days during the summer in Scandinavia, we encounter a sweet folk dream-incubation tradition. On the magical high point of the sun during the festive midsummer night, people who are looking for their beloved can pluck seven different flowers and put them under their pillow before going to bed. When you do this, you will dream about your future husband or wife.

On our journey of meeting those important to the practice of dream incubation, we need to visit the first man who gave me some clues on being with the dream: the great Western dreamworker of the last century, Carl Jung.

Jung was very interested in the Asclepeion healing methods, and he talked often about Asclepius—there are several hundred references to Asclepius in his collected works. Jung also referenced the book by his friend and colleague C. A. Meier, *Ancient Incubation and Modern Psychotherapy*. This book was first published in German in 1949 and deals mainly with the ancient healing tradition of Asclepius and the parallels to Jungian therapy.

When people came to him with a problem, Jung would suggest that they sleep on it, have a dream, and bring it to the analytic hour. It was not as ritualized and formal as in the Greek times, yet it has the same flavor—Jung put dreams back at the heart of the healing tradition. He also used dreams for their diagnostic abilities and prescriptive suggestions.

DISCOVERING DREAM INCUBATION

There are many individuals who have stumbled upon this technique on their own. Dream incubation appears to be an innate human activity. Writer Meredith Sabini has a similar view when she suggests that "dream incubation is a natural spiritual instinct . . . akin to praying or observing omens."[4] I have met quite a few people who told me that they asked their dream a question before going to bed and had remarkable results. When I asked them how they found out the technique, they often shrugged their shoulders and said that they just did this one day and it worked.

CURRENT-DAY RESEARCH

In 2010, *Scientific American* published findings of a study done by Deirdre Barrett, Ph.D., who is an author and psychologist who teaches at Harvard Medical School. She did a research study on dream incubation with her students. Deirdre Barrett asked the 76 student participants to pick a subject of their personal interest, and they had the following results: approximately half of the subjects recalled a dream that they felt was related to the problem. Seventy percent of these believed their dream contained a solution to the problem.[5]

Another interesting finding in her study was that "students were more likely to solve a problem of intense personal interest, or a medical problem, than one of a general or academic nature."[6]

This relates directly to our earlier conversation about which questions lead to productive answers, and which produce no answers at all. Dr. Barrett's research and my own experience suggest that when a person has little emotional engagement with the question or has questions that are not relevant to his or her life path, often the dream seems not to generate helpful responses.

TAKING THE ANCIENT INTO THE PRESENT

This ancient healing and guiding power that millions of people around the world and throughout all ages have connected with is still around. And many non-Western cultures still connect with it regularly. Nothing has changed. The healing god has always been there, is still there, and will always be there. We can also petition the creative and healing powers through creating our own dream incubation ritual.

By looking at these cultures, we have learned some of the structure and rituals we can perform to establish a relationship and connection with our dreams so that we might have our own revelations. In the next chapter, you will find inspiration in the problems, questions, and explorations that people have made in their own dream incubations, so that you may begin your own practice.

CHAPTER 6

HOW DREAMS HELP WITH LOVE, HEALTH, AND PURPOSE

The questions that will give you the greatest reward are those that are deeply personal and close to your heart, but it can be difficult to craft the right question, especially the first few times. To help you on your journey, I am giving you some examples of questions and dream responses to play with. More questions to try out are at the end of this book in Addendum 2. These questions and dreams are meant to spark your own creativity. I hope they inspire you to create beautiful, wild, tantalizing questions!

As you will see, this method of dream incubation is very helpful for dealing with relationship and health issues, yet you can also use it to help you develop a skill, write a book, improve a business, or guide you on your life path. But you need not only use it to solve problems; you can use it to have fun! You can ask for a dream in which you feel free and can fly or one that lifts your spirits. There is nothing wrong with seeking fun for the sake of fun. I can tell you from personal experience that I sometimes get bogged down by the things I want to do—or feel I need to do—and forget to celebrate achievements, take time to relax, and just have fun without a purpose.

You can also dive into the depths of big life questions and explore the nature of reality. Could you contact deceased loved ones? Could you predict what a major headline would be in the newspaper in two weeks, or what it would be like to live in 17th-century Amsterdam? These are wild questions that can only be truly answered from your own direct experience. So, when you are ready for them, take them on!

DEVELOPING TRUST

I was possessed by anxiety from time to time and wondered what I could do about it. I wondered how I could experience and feel more trust in life. I decided to ask my dreams: "How can I trust life more deeply?"

I had the following dream: I was sitting at a table, and I was in the process of working when someone told me that I was good at what I was doing. I nodded and said yes, saying that accomplishing things through hard work was valued and celebrated when I was at the beginning of my career, and it has stayed with me.

The energy of the dream was one of feeling capable, solid, and aware of my positive qualities. I felt that the dream suggested that I could trust more in my own ability to make things happen, and I meditate on and remind myself of that often. I feel it has worked to decrease the visits from my anxiety and help me trust life more deeply.

LOVE AND RELATIONSHIPS

When we are looking for a relationship, it's most help-ful to ask questions that are more internally focused, like: What is one thing I can do to be available for a lover? What can I do to find the love of my life? What are obstacles in me that prevent me from finding love?

There is much to say, and many more dream ques-tions to ask, about the magnificent, exciting, terrifying, and devastating topic of love. We all experience the rich shades, colors, and forms of love differently. Therefore, this example is meant to fan your love flame. It will hope-fully inspire you to fall more in love with your life, find a great partner, or improve an existing relationship through asking your dreams some questions.

Several years ago, I had booked a trip to Rome, as I wanted to visit an Asclepeion dream temple on a little island in the river Tiber. Yet life took another turn as my stepfather was at the end of his life and passed away just before my trip. I postponed my trip and returned home. One of the practices at this specific temple that I had been reading about was dreaming on behalf of someone else—there were many accounts of people who had been able to do so.

On one of my trips, I met Veronica. She told me how she sometimes dreams on behalf of someone else, and even once dreamed about a future lover for one of her friends.

One of her male friends, Roberto, knew about Veron-ica's ability to have profound dreams. Every once in a while, Roberto would joke and ask, "What does my future husband look like?" One evening, he asked again, and Veronica agreed to try to dream for him. And she did dream about someone: "This guy, he had curly hair, and I knew he was Italian, and I heard him speak French in the dream. I knew he did something creative. He was kind of short, yet he had this big head of hair, almost like an afro." The next morning Veronica shared her dream, but Roberto shook his head, saying that the guy didn't sound like his type. "All right," said Veronica, "but one day you will meet this guy."

Several months later, Veronica was having dinner with a friend who said he wanted to set Roberto up with someone. Veronica, remembering her dream, told her friend to ask the potential suitor to come over. When he arrived at the restaurant, Veronica was stunned. It was him! The short man from the dream, with the big afro. He revealed that he was from Italy but lived in Switzerland, and that he was a hairdresser. Veronica texted Roberto and told him to come to the restaurant immediately to meet his husband.

And then they lived happily ever after. Well, okay, they had a relationship that lasted a year and a half, and then they went their separate ways. Nevertheless, the dream showed Veronica Roberto's future lover with great accuracy.

RELATIONSHIPS TO THE WORLD

Could dreams help us connect with the world around us, perhaps with the tree in your yard, or a nearby river? Perhaps you're curious what the hummingbird who visits your window every day has to say, or whether your pet has something to communicate to you. Over the years I have explored this, and here is one example of it.

I once visited the beautiful Antelope Island State Park in Utah. The rocks there are among the oldest—2.7 billion years—in the United States. What must a 2.7-billion-year-old mountain have seen over its lifetime? I decided to take a little bit of the rock home with me, and created a ritual. At night, I talked to the rock, asking the mountain if it had anything to tell me, and put it under my pillow before going to sleep. In the dream, I saw that specific mountain with a deep crater, due to copper mines, in the center. As I observed, I had the distinct feeling of abuse. I felt that the mountain was saying that she was being violated, abused. I both desired and felt obligated to do something with this message.

Carl Jung made an effort to draw ethical conclusions from the images that came to him in day-to-day life. He stated, "It is not enough to gain some understanding of the images and that knowledge can here make a halt. Insight into them must be converted into an ethical obligation."[1]

As a result of this dream, I organized an event on dreams and nature with the Jung Society of Utah. The event's goal was to connect people with nature—outer nature and with their inner nature—and understand the role that dreams can play in those connections. People can have (spontaneous) dreams that show the state of the natural world, as if the trees, the mountain, or the ocean is coming directly to them to share about its own state of being. It is as if our own inner nature and well-being are interdependent on the external natural world. Therefore, we should treat nature well, as we are dependent on it for our own well-being.

I encourage you to do the same—engage with something in nature, whether a tree or flower or hill or animal, or even your pet, your house, or anything meaningful to you. It may have a message of value to impart.

Spiritual explorations

In Tibetan Buddhism, working with dreams is a dedicated spiritual practice, part of a larger goal of reaching enlightenment. They also acknowledge that in the dream state, one can receive spiritual teachings, meet deceased masters, and explore the nature of reality. You can be a spiritual explorer, playing with and testing specific questions.

Mark dresses well, is a hard worker, and is in a loving relationship. However, he had experienced several deaths in his family and decided to participate in a daylong workshop about death called "Living to Die." After the workshop, he decided to ask the dream the following question: "What would be helpful to know about death?"

He had the following dream: "I was in a restaurant sitting at a table and talking with a woman. I look to the right and see, in the middle of the empty restaurant, my deceased father sitting alone at a table, watching us. I am filled with joy when I see him. I wave and ask him to join us. He comes over and stands next to our table. I see him clearly, and I see his face. He then joins us."

Mark felt rejoiced to meet this dream father. Mark took this dream to mean that his father is close to him and watches over him, and the moment he asks his father to be with him closely, he will do so.

Whether you want help with creativity, business, finances, or combating limiting beliefs, you can ask your dream for help. At the end of this book, you will find an addendum with standard questions you can ask your dream. In the next chapter, you will learn how you can best ask your own questions. Life is beautifully mysterious, and only you can develop a question that can help you unravel some of that mystery. Happy explorations!

CHAPTER 7

THE IMPORTANCE OF THE QUESTION

Albert Einstein said: "If I had an hour to solve a problem and my life depended on the solution, I would spend the first 55 minutes determining the proper question to ask. For once I knew the proper question, I could solve the problem in less than five minutes."

Just as Einstein emphasizes taking your time to develop the right question, I echo how important it is to ask a well-formulated question in dream incubation. The quality of your question defines the quality of your answer.

When I work with people who tell me that dream incubation is not working for them because they get confusing dream answers or no answers at all, the first thing we do is look at the way they phrased the question. That is very often the cause of the problem. Let me start with an example of a badly formulated question, resulting in a dream that is hard to understand.

I once facilitated a weekend workshop on dreams in the magical city of Marrakesh, where it feels like you're in the film *1001 Arabian Nights*. One of the participants, a local woman named Faria with beautiful olive skin and warm brown eyes, was conflicted over choosing a roommate. She has a generous nature and a deeply introverted sensitive side, so she is highly susceptible to picking up on the energy of others. Therefore, it was important for her to select an appropriate roommate. She posed the following question to her dream: "Shall I bring in this person as a roommate in my house, or not?"

That is a wrongly formulated question because it has two questions in one. Additionally, these two questions are opposing each other. Can you see why that is problematic? When looking at the dream response, it will be hard to understand which part of the dream answer is responding to the question, "Shall I take her in?" and which part is responding to the "Or not?" Take a moment and consider what kind of dream would answer Faria's question about taking in the roommate or not.

It is much easier to work with a dream that answers a question worded this way: "What is the consequence of taking this woman into my house?" Because then the whole dream applies to the outcome of taking this person in. The ability to imagine a possible dream answer to your incubation question is one of the verification methods of having a good dream question. You can imagine a negative scenario, a positive scenario, or anything in between, and can then see that scenario as a response to your question. We will come back to this verification method later.

To her initial question, Faria had a dream response where she saw triangles moving around; the tips of each of the corners were lit. She couldn't make any sense of that dream. With renewed enthusiasm and a well-formulated dream incubation question, Faria next asked the dream,

"What is the consequence of taking this woman into my house as a roommate?" The next night, Faria had this dream: "I am traveling by car, and the gas runs out. I go to a gas station, but nobody helps me with filling it up. I am very annoyed and angry because nobody is helping me out." (In Morocco, only service staff are allowed to fill your car with gas. Since it is always done for them, people often don't know how to do it themselves.)

She took this dream, in which the main feelings consist of anger, irritation, and lack of help, as a suggestion that those experiences would be the consequences of taking this woman into her house. She decided not to go forward with that potential roommate.

Here you see that a sharper, well-formulated question gives a much clearer and more understandable dream response. Therefore, don't rush when determining what to ask your dream, and how.

THE IMPORTANCE OF ASKING QUESTIONS

The award-winning radio show host and author Krista Tippet said: "Questions elicit answers in their likeness." Before we go to explore what dream incubation question to ask and how to formulate this question, I want to talk more about the importance of asking questions, and not only when it comes to dreams.

Asking questions can generate creative solutions. Asking the right question lies at the heart of discoveries in science, medicine, and philosophy.

The Jungian analyst Marie-Louise von Franz was a specialist in fairy tales and myths. She remarked, "Deliverance as the result of the right kind of question is a universal motif." With the deliverance she refers to the breaking of the spell, the transformation, the redemption. She goes on to say: "In Jungian terms it is an archetypal motif. In fairytales it is usual for the hero who wishes to acquire the treasure to have to fulfill one or more special conditions, on the correct execution of which the result depends. One such condition is the question."[1]

The road to enlightenment in the Zen tradition is paved by koans, riddled questions that are meant to break you open. It is universally recognized that asking the right question is important for bringing you to a new state of consciousness. The tale from the Middle Ages, the Grail legend, is a clear example.

The Fisher King is ill, and it was prophesied long ago that he would be healed when an innocent fool arrived at the court and asked a specific question. The first time our fool Parsifal stumbles into the court, he dares not to ask a question. Everybody is disappointed, and the court has to wait another 20 years until Parsifal finds the castle again. In Parsifal's story the moment he asks the right question is the moment where healing occurs and the whole castle erupts with joy. Jungian analyst Robert Johnson writes, "In Wagner's opera, *Parsifal*, the wounded Fisher King rises at this moment and sings a wonderous song of triumph and power and strength. It is the culmination of the whole tale!"[2]

Asking the right question is so important in these tales because asking a question reveals as much about the person who asks the question as what is revealed by the answer of the other. The right question reveals a person's character, and their authentic intention. The right character and right intention are prerequisites in order for the blessing to be bestowed on the questioner.

The right question in relationships with others (or with yourself) generates intimacy, openness, wonder, and discovery. A great question is the prerequisite for a real conversation. When we are asked specific questions, we come alive. We move to the edge of our known world and are confronted with the unknown. We are being invited to be vulnerable, and that is exactly the place where we connect, where we experience intimacy. Once after a lecture, a friend and participant came to me and asked, "How are you a different presenter today than you were last year?"

I hadn't thought about it before, and so the question moved me to the edge of the unknown. I had to ponder and reflect honestly on how I had changed. There was connection and intimacy with the person asking me the question, because I had to get in touch with my vulnerability in order to reflect. And in vulnerability lies connection.

In our dream incubation quest, it's important to ask great questions: questions that make you ponder, be curious, and unravel new aspects about yourself and your life. That help you bring new creative contributions into the world. You can even ask questions in the dream state, when you become lucid, and experiment in that environment.

Your questions drive your focus, in any state of consciousness, whether you are in this reality or in the dream reality. As Robert Waggoner says: "Your focus serves to select what you experience." If we change our question, we change our experience and the outcomes. Many people ask themselves very disempowering questions, such as, "What is wrong with me?" or "Why can't I lose weight?" or "What does it matter anyway?" Your mind will find answers for your questions, and it will come up with very unflattering answers. These answers will make you feel lousy about yourself, and will often result in unpleasant emotional states and negative directions in your life. If you want a meaningful or more fulfilling experience of life, then you have to be dedicated to asking great questions.

"Asking the beautiful question," as David Whyte would say, can change one's life course. I'll give you an example of a simple question that was posed to me in waking life by a friend and colleague. That question did lead to a dream incubation and made a longtime wish come true.

I remember driving through Amsterdam with my friend. We talked about things we wanted to do in life, and I told him that I always wanted to travel for a year through Asia. I got butterflies in my stomach from that idea. He asked me the stunningly simple question, "And why don't you go?"

An overwhelming silence followed. I noticed my head nod, and then I shrugged my shoulders. I could not answer that question. I knew, undeniably, I could not answer the question of why I would not go. It was silently clear, and in that centered silence in me, the real answer was revealed. There was no real objection that was valid enough for me not to go.

On one of the following nights, I wondered what my dream had to say about this initiative of traveling through Asia for a year. Despite my desire to go, I experienced trepidations, fears of giving up my job, of not having an income, of the potential difficulty of finding a job upon returning, and all the things that could happen to me in a foreign continent. I then dreamed about a guy from high school that I associate with being daring and bold. This dream seemed to me a response to my fear-based objections to this journey. I thought the dream was a suggestion to bring those same qualities to my decision: be bold, be daring.

Three months later, I woke up during an overnight flight and looked out the window over the large green jungle of Thailand. I saw the red sun coming up and knew that this continent was going to be my home for the next year.

That simple question in the car changed the course of my life, for the better. That is the power of the question.

CHAPTER 8

STEP 1: WHAT SHALL I ASK MY DREAM TONIGHT?

The journey of dream incubation starts with the adventurous inquiry of "What shall I ask my dream tonight?" We now know how important questions are, and how an effective question can shape your life for the better. In this chapter, I want to offer you some guidelines to identify and develop your own questions.

WHAT IS A GOOD QUESTION?

A good question opens you up to an exciting—or maybe terrifying—deepening of consciousness, or to trepidation and thrills about your future. To develop a good question invites you to be courageous, honest, vulnerable, and have an ability to sustain tension and fear. It is also an invitation to be kind to yourself. To ask such a question requires you to be open and willing to hear the answer as well.

The word *question* includes the word *quest*, which means "the act of seeking." In medieval romances, *quest* means "a chivalrous enterprise," usually involving an adventurous journey. I like to think of that quest as the underlying spirit in creating a dream incubation question.

A good question has two parts: (1) asking the question and (2) listening to the response. The willingness to listen might seem logical when you ask a question. However, I have seen and experienced many incidents of students not being open and receptive when listening to the answer.

In a workshop on sacred activism and dreams that I facilitated with Andrew Harvey, Andrew came up with a great question: "Where am I a coward?" When I asked the dream that question, I had a genuine desire to know.

In the dream I saw a woman heading toward me. She was someone in my life I felt had betrayed my trust. I was overly friendly when I greeted her. We even had a little dance together. I had her in my arms, leaning back and forth in gracious way, as if I want to charm her. When I woke from this dream, I shook my head. It felt like this dream didn't need much interpretation. I knew this cowardliness in myself: instead of confronting her directly, I was overly friendly. I was aware of fear preventing me, at times, from speaking up or from following a desire I had. Though I was not proud to acknowledge my cowardice, I was willing to work on it.

When we ask dreams for counsel, there needs to be an authentic desire and willingness to listen. Otherwise, why even ask the question? You might get an answer that you'd actively need to hide from yourself. This could lead to a neurotic tension within that would hurt you and inevitably the people around you.

After many years of listening to and developing dream incubation questions, I have found the following four guidelines valuable when creating a question: Is your question alive, is your intention for the larger good, is your question specific, and are you willing to be open to the response?

1. IS YOUR QUESTION ALIVE?

What has been preoccupying your mind today? Which daydreams do you automatically return to? What is stirring up your emotions? Perhaps there is something that you really enjoy fantasizing about, something that angers you, or something that makes you anxious even thinking about it. Any dream incubation question that arises from these areas are great questions, as they are alive.

To develop any of these questions requires a certain courage and dedication to your own life. It might be scary to go after that which you love, and it can be frightening to confront anxiety-provoking feelings. Yet those are the places where you move to the edge of your own self, and that leads to breakthroughs.

The questions that are most alive in you can range from the big questions, having to do with your vocation or intimate relationships, to smaller day-to-day concerns of your own life. After you have asked some big questions, you'll see that day-to-day life allows for many smaller questions that could benefit from some dream support. My sister Akke-Jeanne even likes to ask, "What is the question of the day?"

Have you had an argument with someone today that you're still mulling over? Are you trying to figure something out? Was it a day where you wondered how to be more effective with your time, or how to eat healthier? These are questions you can ask your dreams, and the answers will support you in your endeavors.

What is alive in you could also be seen as what is calling you, or in Jungian terms, the individuation process. A calling invites you to live a more meaningful life, to be connected to the ongoing creation of your own life. In Jung's case the call came in the form of ancestors asking him questions. This is not unlike some African spiritual traditions I have encountered, where the ancestors will visit those with their unanswered and unresolved questions, those who have come to earth with the quest to solve those particular problems.

Sometimes a calling feels like a mandate, a direction one has to go in. At all times, a calling is a question to you; it asks you to participate boldly and generously in the game of life.

Dream incubation questions that are alive generate the best responses. Research from Deirdre Barrett shows that questions that have an emotional connection, and are personally relevant to your life, stimulate dream responses that relate to the question. Dream incubation questions that are not relevant, distant, and general generate less clear or no answer to your question. An alive question will pass the "So what?" test. The question "What did my neighbor have for dinner tonight?" in all likelihood will not pass that test.

HOW TO CREATE AN "ALIVE" QUESTION

Find a place where you can dialogue with yourself without being interrupted. You can write this dialogue out in your journal or just talk out loud to yourself. Just ask yourself this simple question: "What shall I ask my dream tonight?" The first thing that pops up in your mind is what you truly want to ask. Allowing the question to step forward is an act of courage. "A good question comes from our ability to face the unknown," says David Whyte.

If multiple questions present themselves, write them down for future nights. Start with the question that found its way to you first. That is usually the most burning question, the one that will be a generous act toward your future self. According to David Whyte, your future self will be happy that you were willing to ask and face the unknown, because that self is in a better place due to the decision you took today. Sometimes this question is about an emotional topic, or a longing for something that you want to experience. Or it might be a question that has been relentlessly knocking on the door, one that you are afraid to ask—and that you are trying to hide from yourself. These are what David Whyte refers to as the "questions that have no right to go away." These are questions that have to do with your individuation process, or your life path or life contract. If you are afraid, there are several ways to get to the point of asking the courageous question. Later in this chapter, I will explain more on how to do that. Yet the important thing is that you know what you need to ask, and that you work toward formulating it.

2. IS THE INTENTION OF YOUR QUESTION FOR THE LARGER GOOD?

Why do you want to know the answer to your question? Does the answer have a self-serving purpose, or do you want to know something so you can contribute to the world, for the larger good?

There can be different intentions underlying a dream incubation question. For example, the question "What will be the major headline on the front page in *The New York Times*?" depends on several things. Why do you want to know this? What relevance will the answer have to your life? Would you like to brag that you have dreams that can accurately predict the future? In that case, it is a self-serving question. Or are you truly interested in the ability to predict the future? Perhaps you are studying some divination technique such as the tarot or I Ching, and would like to make sure that you work with timelines accurately, and that is why you have asked dreaming's help to teach you about this. Then your intention is for the larger good.

We have seen before that dream incubation questions work best when they are personal and emotionally relevant. Yet some questions about the nature of reality, such as the *New York Times* headline example, are not deeply personal; however, they provide a greater understanding of the world we live in. These questions will deepen one's understanding of the nature of reality, and that is relevant when navigating through this world. This will help you to live in alignment with the world, and that belongs to a positive intention.

A question for the larger good is born of positive intentions. The intention reveals the heart space a person comes from, and as we learned earlier, a heartfelt intention is a prerequisite for triggering a positive and understandable dream response. The right heart space is part of the archetypal motif of asking questions in the quest for healing.

IS THE INTENTION OF YOUR QUESTION BENE-FITING ALL INVOLVED?

Try to develop a question that seems to benefit all participants involved. If you wish to grow your business, you can ask your dream how. In the old days, dreaming would help hunters, from the Icelandic fisherman to the Naskapi, find animals. Often one person would have had especially strong dreams about where to hunt. Yet dreaming would also get upset if one killed more than was necessary for their life. You could also focus your question and add more specificity. Instead of asking, for example, "How can I get more clients?" ask, "How do I get more clients who will benefit from my services?" It is a kinder, more generous question that makes clear that your intention is to benefit all. You can also dedicate some of your dream incubation exploration to the service of others. Martin Luther King said, "Life's most persistent and urgent question is, 'What are you doing for others?'"

At the end of the day, you are the authority on which questions you ask. Even if you don't know if you can ask that question, dreaming doesn't judge. When you make an honest mistake, the response from dreaming seems to be that it appreciates that you gave it a try, and it fully encourages further exploration. We want to remember that dreaming is excited to be engaged; it is on standby waiting to point us into the areas where we need support and answers to our explorations.

3. IS YOUR QUESTION SPECIFIC?

Now that you have identified what is alive for you and you have verified your intention, you want to make sure that your question is specific. To get a dream answer that is valuable and helpful, you need to ask a specific question.

A specific question is clear and focused, and therefore becomes a compass, as it identifies the area that you want to explore. The other very important part of creating a specific question is that you will read your dream response against the question you asked. Your question provides you then with the background to understand your dream.

When developing your question, then, you have to get very specific about what you want to know. A question such as "Tell me everything about this new job opportunity" is too wide and vague. Remember what Krista Tippett said: "Questions trigger answers in their likeness." "Everything about this job" is a lot of information, and how do you decipher what "everything" is? You might get an answer about something that you weren't really interested in, because "everything" about the job could contain many aspects about the job that you already know. A far more focused and specific question is, "What will it be like for me to take this new job opportunity?" More particular questions are, "What do I not see about this new job opportunity?" or "Please tell me something important that I need to know about this job opportunity." You have to think about what you really want to know, and then phrase the question so that it addresses that area of interest.

Bring your best thinking and exploration to the table when you're developing your question. Simply said, will you do your homework before you ask the question? It is only when you have reached the edge of your understanding that you are ready to ask the question. It is not a good idea to ask a question about that new job that you could have figured out easily yourself.

An example of this has to do with a young woman with an aptitude for psychology. She wanted to know which school would be the best for her, and without doing her own research, wanted to ask the dream which university would be best. So, she was advised first to look at the different schools on her own, and then consult the dream only after she had done her part. And armed with her research, she would be able to create a more effective and specific question that would help her determine her best path forward.

Let me give you some other examples of questions and how their specificity makes a difference. If you wish to explore your limiting beliefs, a general question is, "What are my limiting beliefs?" A good start, yet if you think this through, you will see that the dream will then display a larger number of limiting beliefs, and it will be difficult to tease out which part of the dream belongs to which limiting belief. So perhaps you ask, "What is one limiting belief?" You would then get only one limiting belief. Yet you would not know the severity of this belief, whether it is a main limiting belief or just a small one that was active that day. Are there other limiting beliefs that are active and more disruptive, and should they take precedence in the confrontation with these limiting beliefs? If so, you must phrase your question in a way that answers what you really want to know. That question would be, "What is a limiting belief that I have right now?" And if you get even more specific, you can ask, "What is the limiting belief I have right now that is hindering me the most?" Each one of these questions will generate a different answer.

Before you develop your question, ask yourself, what do I really want to know, and after you have developed the question, think through the possible dream responses to see if your question is indeed the correct one.

4. BE OPEN TO THE ANSWER

The willingness to listen to the answer is just as important as the development and asking of the question. You have to have an open state of mind in which you are willing to take the response seriously, work with it, and take an honest look at what it might suggest. I'll address how to be with the dream response and some suggestions on how to work with the dream in Chapter 12.

CHAPTER 9

STEP 2: HOW TO FORMULATE THE DREAM INCUBATION QUESTION

A SMALL CHANGE IN THE QUESTION SETS AVERAGE AND TOP PERFORMERS APART.

In the business world, there was an interesting experiment performed by the Regis Company, where professionals were put in simulators that mimicked some of their business challenges. The researchers determined what made the difference between the top performers and the rest. It was the specific way in which top performers formulated their questions.

The average performers would ask themselves the question, "What should I do?" That is a limiting question. The top performers asked the question, "What could I do?"[1] This tiny difference in formulating the question opens a sea of potential. Because the formulation of the question has a big impact on the outcome, we are going to explore how best to formulate your incubation question and verify if you crafted a good question.

Normally when we think about formulating a question, we think about a question in a written or verbal form. However, not all questions need to be verbal; you can also make an image of your question.

There is another nonverbal way to formulate a dream question: the Embodied Imagination method. With that, you sense into the different experiences of the inquiry and use those body-felt experiences as the incubation. I will describe that further later in this chapter, and in Addendum 1, I give a personal example as well.

1. WHAT WE CAN LEARN FROM THE WAY ELENA FORMULATES THE DREAM INCUBATION QUESTION

Elena, an elegant woman in my dream group, shows a curious mixture of confidence and fragility. She is sharp and fiery but can be ridden with self-doubt and self-deprecation. She tells the dream group that she has started to formulate a dream incubation question. Her dark-brown eyes look at the members of the group, almost wanting some confirmation that this is a good idea. I notice myself nod encouragingly and say, "Please tell us what you are planning to ask."

On the previous dream group evening, we explored the different ways we can ask the dream a question, so the group is eager and ready to help Elena formulate a beautiful question.

Elena says, "I've been struggling a lot with self-love, especially lately," and the sincerity of her words makes each of us feel for her. We also reflect on our own struggles of being kind to ourselves.

Elena continues: "I was making progress for a while, and then some old wounds regarding my father leaving before I was born opened up again recently when I was broken up with. I've been feeling a little hopeless and wonder if those wounds will ever fully heal. I feel like a hurt little girl again, and I have noticed myself lashing out at people and using unhealthy coping mechanisms to deal with the pain."

While Elena looks at the group members, she shakes her head and with some desperation in her voice she says, "I really need to figure out some way to love myself better, a way that hopefully stops some of my destructive feelings and behavior."

One group member, Paul, says that he thinks this is a great topic to create a question for, and he nods at the end of his sentence as if he is agreeing with himself. He looks at Elena and the group and says, "This question is clearly alive, and the intention to love yourself in a better way is a great intention." He addresses the other group members and says, "The topic is specific, Elena really wants to know the answer, and seems open to listening to the dream suggestion." With a smile he says, "So the requirements for what to ask the dream tonight are met." Paul then claps his hands and says enthusiastically, "Let's formulate this dream incubation question together!"

The five dream group participants, including Elena, start to puzzle on formulating the question in the best possible way. Paul leads the charge and starts with suggesting, "Why do I not love myself more?"

By formulating the question in this way, we will get an answer that gives insight into the situation: why she does not engage in more self-love. This is a diagnostic formulation. Yet since Elena already has some sense of why she might not do this, she is really looking for activities she can do to increase self-love. She is looking for a prescription, not a diagnosis.

Because Elena feels she is self-critical, she wonders out loud, "Should I love myself by saying more nice things to myself?"

This is a leading question, and it is not open-ended, which prevents the dream to come up with prescriptions that we haven't thought of. There might be many other ways to love oneself that would be beneficial. Therefore, this question is not well formulated. For Elena we would be better off formulating a more open-ended prescriptive question. The group agrees, and Paul jumps in and asks, how about the following question: "What are the ways that I can love myself?"

It is a pretty good question, but there's a possible danger: by asking for "ways," the dream will present multiple options. That will make it more difficult to figure out what the different ways are. A question like, "What is one thing I can do to love myself?" is more focused, specific, and oriented toward getting one answer. This will make it much easier to understand the dream response, as we can look at the prescriptive activity in the dream and just copy that. If we want more suggestions for self-love, then we can always ask the same question another night.

The slightly quiet yet very imaginative group member Zhang Li feels that Elena already has some aspects she loves about herself. She feels it does more justice to Elena if we would formulate the question as follows: "What is one thing I can do to love myself more deeply?" Zhang Li feels that adding the words *more deeply* would acknowledge that Elena is already engaged in self-love in some ways. She feels that this would allow the dream to show Elena something that she already does but could do more regularly. Plus, it would still allow the dream to come up with any new suggestions for Elena.

There are many ways that people prefer to address this mysterious phenomenon behind the dream in our question. Some people ask the Divine, God, or just Dream, and other people just ask the question. Again, do whatever feels best to you in creating your own relationship with the dream.

Elena agrees with the way the question is formulated, and she says that she likes to address the dream by asking Morpheus, the Greek god of dreams, the question. The final version of Elena's dream incubation question for that night is, "Morpheus, what is one thing I can do to love myself more deeply?"

That evening, Elena engages in the following dream ritual: I look at the stars and say a prayer to Morpheus asking for a dream to come to me that answers my question in a way I can understand. Then, lying down, I repeat my question to myself a few times before relaxing and falling asleep.

Elena then has the following dream response: "I am working in a restaurant and my crush comes in. I go to his table and start giving him all this money. I give money away to other people in the restaurant as well. When I wake up, I hear something in my head telling me to start giving love to myself rather than giving it all away to other people."

The dream is urging Elena to take a look at giving her money—which can symbolize her worth or value—to other people in order to feel loved. Then a dream voice comments on it, suggesting that she starts giving the money, value, love to herself. There is much Elena can start doing now as a result of the dream. She can start to recognize when the impulse comes up to give away, so she can stop that negative reflex for love.

What have we seen in Elena's journey to formulate her question? That there are different types of questions, such as diagnostic or prescriptive, that create different outcomes, and that there are several ways to formulate the question that influence the outcome, such as a closed question versus an open question. We will now explore these and other elements that build up the question in more detail.

2. THREE TYPES OF QUESTIONS: (1) DIAGNOSTIC/PROGNOSTIC, (2) PRESCRIPTIVE, (3) REQUESTS

There are three different types of questions that we can ask the dream: diagnostic/prognostic, prescriptive, or a request.

The first type of question is diagnostic or prognostic. A diagnostic question provides you with an overview of the situation. It is akin to getting a psychological X-ray. This can be very helpful. An example would be, "Why do I struggle with self-love?" or "What is one limiting belief that I have right now?" The dream will then deliver an overview of your problem.

The prognostic question is the expected outcome based on the diagnostic overview. For example, what does it look like for me taking this job, or this house?

Different life circumstances require different types of questions. You could start with a diagnostic question to get an overview, and then ask for a prescription on how to deal with the situation.

Sometimes, one might skip over the diagnostic question and move immediately to the prescriptive question. For example, the diagnostic question, "Why can't I overcome my fear of speaking in public?" gives insight into why you can't. Perhaps you were laughed at when you were young at school during a presentation and that memory creates anxiety. Perhaps the fear is part of your inborn psychological structure. Or maybe the self-diagnosis is false and it's not fear at all, but unease and not knowing how to deal with the positive tension in the body that is present before speaking in public.

Yet knowing why you have it most likely does not solve the problem. Some problems are not solved on the level of understanding. Consider the story the Buddha tells about a man who goes to a doctor with a poison arrow in his arm. The wounded man says to the doctor, "Before you remove the arrow, I want to know who did this to me." Then the wounded man would not have the doctor remove the arrow until he knew the man's job and personal details. Then the wounded man didn't want the doctor to remove the arrow until he knew what kind of material the arrow was made of and what type of bow it came from. This went on and on, and it became clear that the man would die if he continued asking questions. Sometimes just asking how to best take the arrow out of the arm, or the prescriptive question, is better.

The second type of incubation question is a prescriptive question. Elena asked a prescriptive question with, "What is one thing I can do to love myself more deeply?" You ask a prescriptive question when you are looking for a recipe or solution for your problem, or you want medicine for your situation.

The request is the third type of incubation question. The request might be for information, an experience, or help. Examples of request questions are: "I would like to meet one of my spirit guides in the dreamworld tonight" or "tonight during sleep, I would like to experience peace." Another request is, "Dream, please help me work through unresolved anger tonight."

The way you formulate the question will generate different types of answers.

3. GUIDELINES FOR FORMULATING EFFECTIVE QUESTIONS

Before I give suggestions and examples of well-formulated questions, we will take a look at the types of questions that we must try to avoid, namely closed questions, leading questions, and either-or questions.

Closed questions are, for example, yes-or-no questions such as "Dream, should I take this job?" That type of question is limiting and can prevent you from getting valuable information.

Either-or questions are equally ineffective. You might remember Faria from Marrakesh, who asked the either-or question, "Shall I take this person in my house as a roommate or not?" The dream she received was difficult to understand, as the question led to a dream with unclear meanings.

Finally, leading questions don't allow you to get a true, honest answer. When you ask, "Do you also think I should take this job?" there is a bias in your question, and it is better to provide an open space for an answer.

Here are six guidelines that will help you craft your incubation question.

1. Use an open-ended question

Open-ended questions are the way to go when it comes to obtaining information. Open-ended questions allow the dream to respond broadly and present information that you might not have thought about. If you seek your dream's advice on accepting a job offer, a possible house purchase, or what one of your limiting beliefs is, then open-ended questions are the best. An open-ended question would then be, "What might the consequence of taking this job be?"

Here are several examples:

- How can I overcome my fear of approaching this attractive person?

- How does it look for me to buy this house?

- How does it look for me to take this new job?

- How can I lose weight?

2. Ask only one question at a time

"What can I do to find love, and how can I welcome that person in my life?" Two great questions! Just don't formulate them into one dream incubation question. Two questions in one will make it much more difficult to understand the dream response to your question. You will have a hard time understanding which part of the dream is responding to which part of the question.

Another example of how multiple questions can sneak in is by asking a question like, "What are my limiting beliefs?" You are asking for the beliefs, which is plural. To simplify it and make it one question, you could ask, "What is one of my limiting beliefs?" so that the dream answer can focus on one limiting belief instead of clustering in all your limiting beliefs, making it a puzzle for you to figure out.

In this example of the limiting beliefs, you can make the question even more focused. For example, you could ask, "What is the limiting belief that is hindering me the most right now?" This question is precise, sharp, and will lead to a precise dream answer.

3. Split big questions into smaller ones

There are naturally many big life situations that are complex and can't be solved with one question. If you suffer from trauma, health issues, or want to find the love of your life, that is a longer process with multiple questions to guide you along. You must be realistic about time frames and the complexity of your questions. Yet, these big tasks lend themselves very well to be supported by the dream. You can start with a diagnostic question, then ask a multitude of prescriptive questions, and sprinkle in a request here and there. In my dream courses and individual work, I often journey with people for longer periods of time to work on big tasks, ranging from health, vocation, and love to creative projects such as writing a book or finishing a piece of artwork.

4. Word your question precisely

Dreaming responds to your question, so wording is essential. The famous lucid dreamer Robert Waggoner gives an example in his book *Lucid Dreaming: Gateway to the Inner Self* in which he shows that the correct wording of the question within the dream state, while a person is lucid, is very important. Waggoner describes how a painter in a lucid dream asks to look for art. The dreamer finds himself literally looking for art, moving from room to room. The painter learned from the experience, and the next time he asked that question to the dream, he was able to be in a room and look at a piece of art.[2] Precise wording thus plays a very important role in creating an effective question.

British Gallup poll researchers creating a questionnaire have also found that formulating the correct question is vital. In 1986 they did a poll that showed that when they asked whether their country's nuclear weapons made the participants feel "safe," 40 percent of the respondents said yes, and 50 percent said no. The remaining 10 percent had no definite opinion.

Then the pollster changed the question slightly and used the word *safer* rather than *safe*. Then 50 percent of the respondents said that nuclear weapons made them feel safer, and 36 percent said that nuclear weapons made them feel less safe. These percentages reversed just by changing the wording slightly.[3]

5. Choose how to address the dream

When you formulate your question, you must decide whether you want to address the dream or a dream figure. Sometimes people opt to address their incubation to Dream, Mystery, God, Divine, the Great Spirit, or Unknown. In ancient Greek and Roman times, the god Asclepius would be addressed. People often choose to address a certain dream figure that has visited them, an ancestor, a spirit guide, or an animal guide. Other times people just formulate the question and don't use any formal address. This is up to you; this is a personal relationship between you and the source of dreaming, and you can give form to it in the way that suits you best.

6. Verify if you have developed a well-formulated question

After you have developed your question, you must verify that you've formulated it well. To do this, see if you can imagine a dream response to your question.

For example, if I formulated the question, "What would be the most likely consequence of me staying in this job?" I would then need to ask myself if I could imagine dreams that would answer this for me. Whatever your dominant emotion or experience is will give you a clue to what those dreams could mean.

To do this, first I would imagine that it would be a bad decision to stay in the job. In that case I could imagine for a negative answer to have a dream with a car crash. For a dream that would indicate that it would be a positive decision, I could imagine climbing a mountain and enjoying the wide-open vistas. Being able to imagine dream responses makes it more likely that you have formulated your dream well.

If you can't imagine a response, or find that the response would be too complex, then you might need to adjust your question.

IMAGE FORMULATION AND EMBODIED IMAGINATION

There are two other ways that you can also create a question, which are not in a verbal or written form. The first one is through creating images, and the second is through a method called "Embodied Imagination." Let us explore these two methods before moving on to actually consulting the dream.

Image formulation

In the majority of the examples we've introduced thus far, we created a question in words such as, "How can I be kinder to myself?" Yet you can also create a visual of your question and use that instead of spoken or written words. The following is such an example of an image formulation.

Nadia has been married for over 30 years and feels dissatisfied in the marriage. She wonders what is going on in her relationship. She decides to ask her dream before she goes to sleep for help with this issue. She first wonders how to ask the question, and she decides on the following. She looks at the picture taken when she got married. It depicts her hand and her husband's hand together, and the wedding rings on their fingers. Then she imagines a question mark on top of this picture. Before she goes to bed, she asks the source of dreaming to help her and give her an answer to her inquiry. In bed she lies meditating for several minutes on the image of the hands, wedding rings, and question mark. She stays with this question for a bit and then falls asleep.

She has the following dream: "I am new at a workplace where only women work. They are sitting inside at long rows of desks. I am going to be getting my own desk in a room that I will share with several other women. The workplace has the feel of the 1950s. Then I read the contract for my work and see that I earn $6 dollars an hour. That is under minimum wage! I want to talk to my manager about this." That is where the dream ends.

She and her husband are in the habit of sharing their dreams, so this morning when she wakes up after having this dream, she shares the dream without mentioning the question to her husband. The husband picks up on the part of the dream where the woman is underpaid for her work, and asks her, "Is there any area in your life where you feel undervalued?"

She says yes, and that she has a pretty good idea which area that is.

EMBODIED IMAGINATION

Robert Bosnak's method of Embodied Imagination is very effective but can be difficult to do on your own. With Embodied Imagination, you experience the elements of your question with your body. For example, you are stuck in writing your novel. You first experience the sense of staring at the blank page of the book you are writing. Then, through a guided method, you enter into the blank page so that you can experience the blank page itself. You hold these two experiences, and that forms the incubation question. For a more detailed description, see Addendum 1 at the end of this book, where I describe an incubation Bosnak did with me.

Now that you know how to formulate the question, let's look at what you can do on the evening that you ask the question to increase the likelihood of a strong dream response.

CHAPTER 10

STEP 3: THE DREAM NIGHT AND ASKING THE QUESTION

After you have identified the topic that is alive for you and chiseled it into a well-formulated question, you are ready to consult your dream. The Dream Night has arrived, and the time of asking the question is one of anticipation, hope, doubt, and excitement. Is there something you can do on the Dream Night to increase the likelihood of a helpful dream?

Meredith, who lives in the Salt Lake City valley, asked her question in a creative way on the Dream Night. She says: "I first wrote in my journal about the situation surrounding my question. Then I wrote down three things I'm grateful for, because gratitude seems to be helpful in this process, at least for me. Following that, I wrote down the question in my journal and placed a crystal that I have, called a Shamanic Dream Stone, over the question. When I went to bed, I held the crystal in my hand while thinking of my question, then put the crystal under my pillow and continued thinking about the question as I went to sleep."

Meredith asked the dream question quite elegantly, which increased the likelihood of her receiving a helpful dream. Why that might be the case is something we will discuss later in this chapter. We can distill an effective and easy two-step process from the way Meredith asked the dream her question:

1. Write your question down before you go to bed.

2. Engage in a ritual.

EXPLORING THE TWO-STEP PROCESS OF ASKING YOUR DREAM A QUESTION

The first step, to write your question down before you go to bed, is essential. You can easily forget what you asked, but since you must work with the dream as a response to your question, it's important to record the question. For example, if you forgot whether you asked, "What is going on in my relationship?" versus "What can I do about my relationship?" then you don't know what the dream is answering. In this case, the first question will produce a diagnosis and the second will provide a dream prescription. If you forgot exactly what you asked, then you can't work the dream.

I learned this myself several times the hard way. I would have a pressing question and would be convinced I would remember what I asked the next day. I would wake up, having had a delightful dream, and then couldn't say for sure what the exact phrasing of my question was. I felt kind of silly, as I thought that if it were important to me I would have remembered the question well. Over time I learned that this is a human tendency rather than a personal one, as my clients and people in my dream groups have encountered the same problem of forgetting the exact phrasing of their dream incubation question.

The other reason to write down your question is as a signal to the dream that this issue or question is important to you. The more the dream knows that you are serious about it, and that you are willing to make some effort to receive an answer, the more helpful your dream becomes.

THE SECOND STEP: ENGAGE IN A RITUAL ON THE DREAM NIGHT

In order to get the most beneficial response, you want to express your desire for a helpful dream through engaging in a ritual. A dream ritual is an activity that aims at nourishing the relationship with the dream and the dream beings, and it's a way to invite dream, spirit, and the Mystery into your life.

Any activity can therefore become a ritual if it is done with the intent, focus, expectation, beliefs, emotion, and willpower to be in touch with spirit.[1] When a ritual is alive, spirit is involved. When a ritual is dry and boring, it lacks the participation of dream and spirit—and technically does not even qualify as a ritual. If this occurs, you must change the activities so you will feel inspired again when you do the ritual.

Don is a writer and got stuck in his novel, so his ritual on the Dream Night was to put an empty piece of writing paper next to his bed and ask for inspiration to fill that page with creative and tantalizing words. Elena, whom we met in the previous chapter, engaged in the following manner: "I looked at the stars and said a prayer to Morpheus (the Greek god of Dreams and Sleep) asking for a dream to come to me that answers my question in a way I can understand. Then, lying down, I repeated my question to myself a few times before relaxing and falling asleep."

In Chapter 6, I shared that I once asked a question to a mountain. During my visit, I searched and selected a little rock to take home. I put that rock under my pillow as part of my dream incubation ritual.

These are all personalized rituals in which we actively relate to Spirit. We put in effort, show that we are interested, and communicate that we need support.

Many spiritual and religious traditions advise dream incubation as a form of getting help from the Divine and have their own prescribed rituals on how to go about asking the question.

In the following dream incubation ritual prescription from Hinduism, you'll see several features that align with those in other dream incubation traditions. The Chandogya Upanishad suggests "to prepare a special mixture of herbs, honey, and curd on the night of the full moon, to pour offerings of ghee into a fire while praising various gods, to drink the whole of the mixture, and finally to lie down behind the fire, remaining silent and unresting."[2]

This ritual consists of engaging in a specific activity (in this case, creating a special drink), making offerings and sacrifices, praising, and praying to the gods, and sleeping in a certain place.

For your own Dream Night ritual, you can follow a ritual from one of the dream traditions, or you can reinvent and personalize it.

HOW TO CREATE YOUR OWN DREAM NIGHT RITUAL

The secret sauce: your own imagination and heartfelt effort

"Last night I created a dream pocket consisting of a small cotton bag filled with sage flowers, a dove's feather, and my dream question. The sage was from my garden and gathered by moonlight. The dove's feather was a gift left by the air during the light of day. My dreaming question was written on notepaper and tied with a purple silk ribbon. The dream pocket was placed beneath my pillow and I lay quietly on my back thinking of my dreaming question until sleep came."

This was a beautiful Dream Night ritual from Carly, a teacher at a high school with soft, kind eyes, a gentle voice, and a rich imagination. She had been participating in one of my dream circles. This ritual absolutely invites the Dream to participate in your life and communicates that you are interested in its response. Carly said that she came to all of this by just following her imagination. That is exactly what you want to follow in creating a ritual—your own imagination. See what your fantasy comes up with. What you start imagining to be a good ritual usually is one. Your own imagination combined with heartfelt effort will no doubt lead you to create a special ritual.

The effort that comes from the heart is what really counts. This effort cannot be measured, yet it is felt by the dream for its genuine intention, as it is a real expression of love. You can do something like read a poem, create something unique for the dream, engage in a prayer, meditate, burn a candle, or make an offering. Heartfelt effort establishes a situation in which the dream is likely to respond in a more favorable or effective way.

Sometimes when you are asking a big and important question, you might postpone the Dream Night a little, and take several days to build up to it. In other words, you increase the length of the pilgrimage phase and stay at the temple to prepare. This all helps to build up desire and shows your earnestness, which translates into building a stronger relationship with Dream, and increases the likelihood of getting a helpful response.

Another practice that many spiritual traditions have carried out to increase the efficacy of the dream response is to sleep in another location. Often one would go to a temple or a grave of a saint or sleep in a cave or some sacred place. It takes heartfelt effort to travel to such a place and spend the night there. Some of these special places might also have an energy that is favorable for connecting with the dream. If you have a very important question or request, and you have the option to sleep at such a special place, then do so. It is a statement to the dream that you are very serious about your quest.

The secret sauce to a successful dream incubation ritual is following your imagination and putting your heart into it. Yet there are also several ingredients that different people and different traditions have used in cooking up their rituals.

THREE INGREDIENTS FOR A SUCCESSFUL DREAM NIGHT RITUAL

I have learned and tested these three ingredients in my own dream incubation explorations, as well as with my patients and dream group participants over the years.

And due to their high efficacy, spiritual traditions around the world prescribe these ingredients in their suggested dream incubation rituals as well. As a good dream incubation chef, you can use these ingredients to your liking.

1. Create a symbolic ritual.
2. State your case, and include an offering and/or sacrifice.
3. Meditate in bed.

CREATE A SYMBOLIC RITUAL

You can create something that has to do with your specific question or problem. Any symbolic presentation of your question is a great way to communicate. Consider Don, the writer, with his empty page when he got writer's block. A Brazilian woman named Andressa had been searching for a relationship for a decade after her divorce, so she painted a beautiful heart for her love question. When Mark, a gifted and attentive therapist with piercing eyes, was stressed about his finances and whether he had enough patients, he put a coin under his pillow and asked a money-oriented question. These are all symbolic, specific rituals relating to the question. Use your imagination and create something that meaningfully connects to your question.

STATE YOUR CASE, AND INCLUDE AN OFFERING AND/OR SACRIFICE

It helps to communicate your desire for an answer to the dream by stating your case. Tell the dream why this answer is important to you. State how this will help you and the people around you. How will the answering of your question contribute to your being kinder, or more generous, or a more fulfilled person who shares their gift with other people?

This is not a begging exercise, and I call it "stating your case" for a reason. With confidence and energy, you state (preferably out loud) your case.

You might also want to offer something while you state your case. You can do a little offering such as burning a candle or pouring some water as a libation.

Also state what you plan to do when you receive a helpful answer. A woman who asked the dream for help with her diet told the dream that if she had a helpful dream, she would buy a healthy dinner for a homeless person in the next week.

In his online course "Inviting Creative Genius into your Life"[3] on JungPlatform.com, Robert Bosnak speaks about the time he worked with a person on a dream incubation. This person made the vow that if the response was helpful, she would donate a thousand shoes to a village in India where people suffered from a particular disease that was aggravated by not wearing shoes.

In the Asclepeion tradition, there was the element of sacrifice. When the patient was healed immediately, or finally had regained his health, he was bound to offer a thanksgiving and to fulfill whatever vows he had made. The offerings of thanks to Asclepius did not necessarily consist of animal sacrifices. In exchange for the fulfillment of their wishes, people could give almost anything: money, incense, laurel, olive shoots, oak leaves, songs, brass rings, candles.[4]

Asclepius seemed not to be interested in extravagant offerings, however. It was simply important to him for people to be thankful and follow through on their promises.

By thanking the dream for its engagement and following up, you also continue to stay related to the dream. You ask the dream something, the dream responds, then you offer thanks—there is a dialogue with Dream, an ongoing interaction that can extend beyond the single nighttime dream experience. In this way, dream incubation is not just a one-time engagement with the dream, but part of a larger tapestry of being, woven into an ongoing dialogue with Dream.

MEDITATE IN BED

Before you fall asleep, lie in bed and meditate about your dream question for several minutes. This is one of the more helpful ingredients for triggering a dream that provides clear answers. Several Buddhist traditions believe that your emotional and mental state just before you fall asleep moves into the night and dreams. It is popular to practice compassion before bed to ensure prolonged states of compassion through the night.

Amelia is curious, a spunky dance teacher, and moves a lot when she talks. In one of our sessions, she told me that she was reading a short story in bed before falling asleep. However, she fell asleep two pages before finishing that story. In her dream she found herself back in the story as an active participant. She continued to dream further into the story. She woke up from an interesting dream adventure and had finished the short story in her sleep. She then also read the actual ending of the book and felt that her dream had produced an even better ending.

On the Dream Night, it helps to move into a relaxed state when lying in bed and considering your inquiry for several minutes. There are several ways that you can do this meditation. You might want to repeat the question for several minutes as a mantra. You can also start by creating mental pictures of your question. For example, if you want to purchase a house, imagine a house. You can sense into your question and notice where in your body you feel the sensations related to your question, and just be aware of and stay with those particular sensations.

Any form of meditation that fits you and your question at that moment is a great way of engaging in the dream incubation ritual.

A REVIEW OF THE PROCESS

It is an exciting evening when you enter the Dream Night, the night on which you ask your dream your question. You can ask the Dream the question through following the easy two-step process. First write down your dream question before you go to bed, and then use your secret sauce and ingredient to create a dream incubation ritual. I hope you will enjoy your process of asking!

CHAPTER 11

STEP 4: SLEEP, DREAM, RECORD

Gerald hears his alarm clock beep, and his sleepy hand moves to the right, over the stacked books on his nightstand. His hand knows where to find his phone, and he shuts off the alarm. His other hand moves through his curly hair, and he stretches out. Then he remembers he had asked the dream a question the night before. He quickly tries to recall what it was that he dreamed. For a moment, he can't remember it, and he closes his eyes again and lies quietly in the same position. "Ah, there is a fragment," he notices, and he allows the fragment to play itself out. Then another fragment reappears, and then the whole dream comes back to him. He knows that he must repeat the dream several times to himself so that he remembers it well.

Gerald is deeply introspective and has always been fascinated by his inner life and dreams. From an early age, he had the routine of writing down dreams in a dedicated dream journal upon waking, while still sitting in bed.

After all the hard work of creating a beautiful question, engaging in a dream incubation ritual, you want to capture your dream. It is very important that you, just like Gerald, immediately record your dream when you wake up. At night your short-term memory is not active, and that is the main reason why you don't remember much from your night of sleep. The short-term memory just slowly comes online in the morning and makes remembering and storing the dream also more difficult. Most of us know the experience of having a dream and being sure that we will remember it later, and not even 10 minutes later it has just completely evaporated. After so many years of writing down dreams and knowing so well that the dream evaporates, I sometimes still fall into the trap of thinking that I will remember the dream and postpone writing it down immediately. Of course, the negative consequence is that I lose the dream and my answer to my incubation question.

Gerald had bought a special dream journal and pen, which would only be used for recording dreams. This gesture indicates to the dream that you take the relationship seriously, that it is important to you, and that you put in heartfelt effort to record it. Gerald thinks of the dream as a sacred experience that has helped him so much in his life. He wants to make sure the dream knows he is grateful for their relationship. On the first page of his dream journal, he wrote a personal message to the dream, describing how he wants to live a dream life and contribute to the world, and humbly asking the dream to support him.

Some people like to record their dream in a voice message—no matter how, recording your dream is essential. What I have noticed is that for the people I have worked with, very few ever write out the dream on paper after they record it as a voice message on their phone, and so it remains a captured dream, locked up in a phone. If you do record the dream digitally, try to make sure it gets into a dream journal.

While Gerald is still sitting in his bed, he writes the dream down in the present tense. Then he goes back to the beginning of the dream and writes down what he experiences. "I am standing on the shore of an island, waiting for a boat to bring me back to the mainland. I have taken a holiday and realize it is time to go home again."

You probably felt an aliveness and immediacy to Gerald's dream and that is because it is written in the present tense. Therefore, write down the dream as if you are experiencing the dream right now, and describe what you experience in the present tense. You can write out the storyline of what happened and include your feelings and experience in it. This last part is crucial. Very often people write objectively what they experienced but forget to include how the experiences made them feel. And sometimes your answer lies within your dream feelings.

By doing it that way, the experience feels more accessible and the emotions in the dream are closer to you. It will allow you to get a better sense of what is going on in the dream, and it could allow you to reenter the dream.

Gerald looks at his wife, Karen, who is still asleep. They have been together for a decade, and he is still enamored with her. Her closed eyes move rapidly from left to right and right to left, meaning she is in the REM (rapid eye movement) stage of sleep. Karen tosses and turns, possibly having an intense dream experience.

He knows that in about one hour she will go through the same process of waking up and capturing her dream. They both love to see what the dream brings, and sharing their nightly adventures with each other is deeply intimate. He smiles when he thinks that she will call him later this morning and ask him about his dream.

Years ago, when Karen met Gerald, she did not have such an active dream life. Actually, she didn't remember her dreams at all. There was a nightmare from her childhood that she could still vividly remember, but for years she had not remembered a dream. She even thought that she had just stopped dreaming. Because of Gerald's ongoing fascination with his dreams, she became interested in her own dreams, and she wondered if she would dream again. Gerald told her not to worry. He said: "Everybody dreams for several hours a night, and the way to activate dream recall is simple. It comes down to getting a dream journal and a pen, putting it next to your bed, and writing down whatever you can remember directly upon waking."

That is indeed the proven method, and engaging in the dream incubation process further increases your ability for dream recall. If you don't have a dream the first night, don't worry. In that case, it is often helpful to write down the emotions you felt when you woke up, and where in your body you felt them. That in and of itself sometimes gives you some information, and it helps to trigger dream recall for the next nights. Continue to repeat the process, and within days you will have a dream.

Gerald had already left the house when an hour later, Karen woke up. Despite getting enough hours of sleep, she often struggles for the first 10 minutes after waking up. She had a series of intense dreams the night before. She woke up during the night and remembered two dreams, and now she remembers another four.

Some people report that they are flooded with dreams and don't know what to do with that. If this is the case and you don't have the energy and time to write them all down, you can tell the dream that you will write down the first dream and take that as a response to your dream incubation question, or the first three dreams. You can establish your own relationship and agreements with your dream. Again, this process of dream incubation is your personal relationship to the dream.

Sometimes people ask me if they have to write down a dream in the middle of the night—this is up to you. Unless it is a very intense dream, I tend to refrain from waking up fully and writing it down. If I have to put the lights on to calm myself down, though, then I will record the dream.

THE IMPORTANCE OF SLEEP

When Karen and Gerald met a decade ago, they were both burning the candle on both ends. They wanted to do everything in life, and well—have a great relationship, excel at work, be talented at their hobbies—so they cut down on sleep. After they had experienced the honeymoon phase of their relationship, Karen started to notice that Gerald was moody from time to time, and that she couldn't focus as intensely and for as long as she used to. She also felt that she wasn't learning things as quickly either. Moodiness, lack of focus, and not retaining information well are just three of the symptoms of not sleeping enough. Karen and Gerald talked about it, and then studied the impact of lack of sleep. They learned that not only did it contribute to moodiness and lack of focus, but it negatively impacted the immune system and metabolic system. Research indicates that people who nibble away at their sleep now pay the price later—they are more likely to die younger. The takeaway is that if you sleep enough, your health improves, your immune system can function optimally, you can more easily stay in shape, you can live longer, you are sharper, you can learn new skills more quickly, and in general, you will be more resilient—and happier.

RECORDING YOUR DREAM IS AN ACT OF FRIENDSHIP

As I said earlier, this technique of asking a question to the dream is much more than just a one-time communication; it is an ongoing dialogue. You develop a question, create a ritual in which you connect with dreaming, then the dream responds, and then you respond by writing down the dream. After that you will begin working through the dream and teasing out the answer you wished for. That is what we will explore in the next chapter.

CHAPTER 12

STEP 5: HOW TO WORK WITH YOUR DREAM

"It worked! It worked!" yelled Imani, almost tripping over her feet while running into the room. She had just turned 15 and had grown a lot in the last year. She had the awkward movement that teenagers often had. Her eyes were full of excitement as she joined her mom, Hannah, her dad, Terrell, and her older brother, Tommy, at the breakfast table.

The night before, the whole family had decided to ask their dreams for guidance. Terrell had just finished writing down his dream when Imani ran into the room. Hannah did it while she was still in bed. Tommy, though, was a little disappointed. He couldn't remember any dreams from the previous night.

Hannah had been following a dream circle and learned the incubation technique. Her dream success had inspired the family to start doing dreamwork. In fact, Hannah noticed that the family had grown closer due to sharing dreams in the morning.

They had all, for different reasons, asked the dream a question for guidance in their life. Terrell had had pain in his hand for months now, and had seen an alternative doctor. The doctor had done some muscle testing on him, and Terrell had left the office with a stack of natural medicine pills. He had been skeptical and asked a prognostic question on what it would look like for him to continue to visit this doctor.

Hannah had been experimenting with questions, and the question that was alive for her the day before was the question for a dietary prescription. She had asked, "Dreaming, what is a food that you recommend I eat regularly?" Imani had worked with her mom on formulating the question that was most emotionally pressing for her, and together they had come up with the diagnostic question, "What is one limiting belief that I have, right now, that hinders me the most?"

Tommy, 23, had just finished his studies and decided to ask where to find a suitable job.

Now they were all sitting at the breakfast table, ready to work on their dreams.

How to work on the incubation dream? We will see what kind of interesting and surprising dream responses Terrell, Hannah, and Imani had, and how they worked on their dreams. And learn what to do when you don't have a dream, like Tommy.

We'll start with four guidelines for working with incubation dreams, and then you'll get a dreamwork recipe for how to work with the dream itself.

Four dreamwork guidelines and a recipe for an incubation dream

I am meeting Terrell in a café in Hollywood, the day after a lecture I gave in LA. I look at the wide variety of cakes they have behind their counter and force myself to just order a cup of rooibos tea. The palm trees, the gentle, dry climate, the sunshine in this place have a lush feel. Terrell and I decide to sit outside on the patio. He is rugged and sensitive. Terrell grew up in a rougher part of LA, raised by a single mother, and joined the army the moment he was able to. Soon after he left the army, he met Hannah and fell in love. They have now been married for 25 years. Now Terrell is an executive at a high-tech company and interested in being the best version of himself; he feels that dreams help him with that.

Terrell likes to test things for himself before he adopts them into his life. He is reflecting on the different dream interpretation books on the market that he has been reading recently. He feels that many of them contradict each other. He shakes his head and says, "One culture explains that the snake is a symbol of healing, and another culture says the snake is a symbol of seduction and the devil. Confusing."

What Terrell has noticed is true. You cannot make a general theory of dreams.[1] You cannot assign fixed meanings to dream images. Different cultures interpret certain symbols differently according to their tradition—all interpretations are valuable, but when faced with so many possibilities, one can get confused. On a personal level, too, people have different associations with dream images. For example, two people dream about a horse. One person has had very positive experiences with horses; she grew up with them. For her that horse might represent love or comfort. The other person was once hurt by a horse and is therefore afraid of them. Dreams are creations of your specific mind and your unique life. Some dream figures resist interpretation,[2] saying that making an abstraction of them or turning them into some meaning system takes away from their living reality. They want to be related to, tended to, and engaged with.

Dream interpretation books have their limitations. Carl Jung said, "The art of interpreting dreams cannot be learned from books. Methods and rules are good only when we can get along without them." Therefore, I want to give you four guidelines, plus a dreamwork recipe for working with dream incubation dreams. Then by practicing, playing, listening to the suggestions, and testing the techniques, you will develop your own art of working with the dream.

FOUR GUIDELINES

First Guideline: Treat the dream as a friend and wise counselor.

When you ask your dream a question, do so as if you are asking a kind, creative, and intelligent phenomenon a question. This phenomenon has a broad overview of your situation, knows you intimately, has tremendous healing powers, and is "interested in helping and educating."[3]

Jung said: "Together the patient and I address ourselves to the two-million-year-old man that is in all of us. In the last analysis, most of our difficulties come from losing contact with our instincts, with the age-old forgotten wisdom stored up in us. And where do we make contact with this old man within us? In our dreams."[4]

Out of this idea of friendship and respect for this "two-million-year-old man," follow the second guideline:

Second Guideline: Treat each dream response to your question as an answer.

A surprisingly high number of incubation dreams are clear and relatively easy to understand. However, what about the dreams we don't understand? We may think they have nothing to do with our question. Those are the dreams that make us doubt whether this whole incubation thing works at all.

Sometimes the dream doesn't make sense to our habitual consciousness. The dreamworker Robert Bosnak thinks that could be because the incubation dream contains new information that is alien to the individual, and therefore, the dreamer doesn't recognize it as valuable. The ego can even find the new information frightening. Dreamwork group participant Jeffrey was writing a book, and he asked "to meet the spirit of the book." In the dream he sees a massive ball of fire. He is afraid for this ball and knows it can burn down everything. He is also afraid that it will alienate him. We then work the dream through the method of Embodied Imagination, in which the dreamer gets to experience the ball of fire. Jeffrey sensed into the ball of fire and was able to get a bird's-eye view and experience the ball of fire as an instinctive intelligence. The ball of fire was powerful, forceful, fierce, yet also deeply intelligent. As if it was the force that wanted to become the book, and that it would help the writer get the book into the world. It became clear here that what appeared really frightening and overpowering to Jeffrey was the new form of intelligence that appeared in the dream and could be helpful to him.

I have heard this comment about dreams that initially make no sense often from workshop participants or patients. Yet they also say that sometimes after they wrote

down the dream it started to make sense. Or if they puzzled on it and no meaning showed up, it would start to
dawn on them later during the day.

Let me share an incubation dream that I had several
years ago that I initially didn't understand. I had gone
to the Lava Hot Springs, which are located in Idaho, just
over the border from Utah. These hot springs were an old
sacred place to the Native Americans. They used to come
there to bathe, and to have ceremonies to thank and celebrate the Great Spirit for the healing waters. These days,
the hot springs are mainly a pleasant tourist attraction,
and especially in the summer people come here to party.
I have come to enjoy the warm waters, and hope to be
touched by their healing powers and encounter some of
the magic of this place. After enjoying an afternoon and
evening in these waters, I go to the little inn where I stay
and decide to ask the hot springs if they have a message
for me. I have the following dream: "I am at the party of a
friend of mine, and it is at her parents' house. Her parents
are rather conservative, religious, and against drinking
at their place, and anyone having sex before marriage in
their home would be completely out of the question. In
the dream her parents are away for the night, and it is a
very wild party. The next morning at 10 A.M., I help clean
up. The house is large, yet there are beer cans, bottles, and
a mess almost a foot high all over the place. I also know
that people had sex at the party, and I can hardly believe
the disaster this party has created."

Initially when I woke up, I thought that this dream
had nothing to do with my question. I was hoping or
expecting some spiritual message, something more sacred.
I was tempted to dismiss the dream. But I did write it
down, deciding that at least on one level the dream would
respond to my question.

I started to think about it, and after a while, I came up with a possible answer. The Lava Hot Springs might be communicating that they are the beautiful home in the dream. The religious owners of the home in the dream would be devastated when they found out the debauchery that had occurred in their home. In the same way, the hot springs felt violated—they have not been paid the respect they deserve. That message would make a lot of sense to me, especially since I could see the difference of the place between being a sacred place with ritual and ceremonies as it was in the old days versus the party style of the current days. The Lava Hot Springs would understandably be upset.

The dream above gave me an answer that I didn't expect, and that was perhaps also one of the reasons that it took me a bit of work. It is easy to overlook an answer if it comes where you didn't expect it to be. This Lava Hot Springs dream initially didn't make sense to me, yet after a bit of engagement with the dream, I came to an answer that seemed sensible to me. When we don't immediately understand our dream, we need to allow the dream presence to be with us. Perhaps they will reveal themselves more during the day.

If you did not understand the answer, you can always ask for another dream to clarify the response. However, there is a big difference between not liking the answer and not getting the answer. If you simply don't understand the answer after a real effort of puzzling on the dream, you can continue to dialogue with dreaming. You could say: "Dreaming, I am flattered that you think I would get this message, yet I don't understand it. Can you make the message even simpler?"

Therefore, this second guideline is to take the relationship with dreaming seriously, and treat the incubation dream you receive as a valid response to your question.

Third Guideline: Multiple layers of meaning and several different ways to work with a dream.

There is no one perfect interpretation or way of working with your incubation dream. A dream can speak to multiple layers of meaning at the same time. Therefore, you don't have to stress about whether the interpretation fits just right, or whether the answer you received is the correct one. A dreamer once spoke to me about searching for a diamond ring in the dream. She felt it had to do with feeling special, and also about her desire to find a partner.

There are several ways of working with the dream. You can work on the meaning of the dream, experience the dream, talk to dream figures, or follow up with a ritual to honor the dream. In this chapter we'll focus on looking at the structure of the dream and following the dream up with a ritual.

Fourth Guideline: Use common sense!

When you ask your dream a question, it has your best interest at heart. The Mystery will therefore not spontaneously start suggesting harmful activities, like engaging in drug activity or robbing a bank. Common sense will tell you that those activities will make you less fulfilled in this life.

I once had the following incubation dream as a response to the question on what type of food I should eat for optimum health. "I am at a beach in Florida—great warm weather, sunshine—and I am sitting in a chair drinking some coconut with whiskey."

You could then say that I need to drink coconut with whiskey on a regular or daily basis, if that is good for me. However, common sense would say that drinking whiskey daily is in general not healthful, and definitely not for me. On top of that, I don't really like whiskey. I had that dream in a time frame where I didn't take much time off and would focus on work and was not drinking much already. So, I took it to mean that once in a while, I should take a break, enjoy a holiday, and relax with a "coconut and whiskey."

A DREAMWORK RECIPE

One of the more fun, exciting, and challenging aspects of dream incubation has arrived: how to work with the incubation dream. These instructions describe how you can work with any dream, not just an incubation dream (step three, however, is only applicable when you ask the dream a question). Here is the recipe:

The Four Steps of the Dreamwork Recipe

1. Dreamwork is teamwork

2. What is the dream experience?

3. Read your dream against against your incubation question

4. Ritual and realization

Step 1: Dreamwork is teamwork

My first suggestion is to invite the Dream, the source of dreaming, and the dream inhabitants to be part of the dreamwork. Usually, this invitation works best by creating a ritual. This can be as small and simple as lighting a candle, meditating for a moment, and asking the dream and its inhabitants to be present for the dreamwork. You can invite your dream team to be present. That can include Jung's "two-million-year-old man," your intuitive self, a spirit guide, or your ancestors; or you might just be asking the team to help your brain focus on the work.

It is more fun to do the dreamwork together than alone, and remember, the dream is interested in helping you. While you engage with the dream, the dream team will talk to you through intuition, giving you thoughts and ideas that pop into your mind, giving you the feeling when you are on the right path or wrong path.

Dreaming is always present, and nurturing an ongoing relationship with it will be helpful for the relationship and friendship you are building with the dream itself.

Step 2: What is the dream experience?

After you have written down your dream, start with the question about the dream: "What was my experience?" This question is different from "What does the dream mean?" With this question, you look at what the structure of the dream is, and what the dominant feelings and emotions are in the dream.

This approach has roots in the philosophy of other dreamworkers. Robert Bosnak suggests starting with a structural analysis of the dream. Stephen Aizenstat suggests asking the question "What is happening?" Carl Jung compares dreamwork to a play or drama; it's up to you to figure out the beginning, development, and ending. These questions by Bosnak, Aizenstat, and Jung are all inquiries into the structure of the dream.

Once you have the general structure of the dream recorded, move to the second step of discovering what the dominant feelings and emotions in the dream are.

The third step is to ask yourself if the dream is literal or if it is symbolic, or metaphorical. Say you are in a dream walking on a road, and you come upon a fork in the road. You can go left or right, but you must decide the way forward. Does that then sound like a metaphor?

In summary, there are three steps to creating a full picture of the dream experience:

a. What is happening (the structure of the dream)?

b. What are the main emotions and feelings?

c. Literally or symbolically/metaphorically?

An interesting experiment

Let's review some examples. Terrell looks at me after I explain the dreamwork steps. He asks, "Can you give me an example of how you have ever worked with a dream on the question, 'What is the experience?'" One recent dream pops into my mind, one that I describe to Terrell as an interesting experiment.

I had recently been on a date with a woman named Pamela, and we had spoken about dream incubation. When you date me, you'll end up talking about dreams sooner or later, I say to Terrell, smiling. At the end of the evening, Pamela said, "Shall I ask the dream the question, what it would be like for me to continue to date you?" I thought that was very clever, and it made me curious about her dream response.

The next day she sends me her exact question and the resulting dream response. Her question is, "What would a relationship look like with Machiel?"

Pamela has the following dream: "We are at the same place as last night, and at the same table. The waitress brings over chicken wings, and a drink for Machiel. I don't remember Machiel ordering, so it is weird that a drink just shows up for him. Then Machiel is feeding me and having me drink his drink. He even cuts the food and holds the glass when I drink."

Naturally I hope you are already puzzling and wondering what this dream could indicate. Yet what we miss in the description is the experience of the dreamer; we don't know enough about the emotions and feelings she had in the dream. It is crucial to know how it feels for Pamela to be sitting with Machiel. Is it pleasant, unpleasant, or neutral? How did she feel about the food and drink? Did she like being fed? We cannot derive that information from the concrete description Pamela provided.

In one of my dream groups, I shared this dream experiment, and one of the participants said that she would not like to be fed in that way. In that moment the dreamwork participant started to fill in the experience of the dreamer—Pamela—with her own feelings. We should try to stay away from that. It is the dreamer's dream, not ours.

Pamela's emotional experience was as follows: "I ate, but I don't remember if I liked it. The drink was wine or champagne, and I liked that. In general, the experience of being with Machiel was good; it didn't make me nervous. I do remember being caught off guard by the food showing up, then by being fed."

Pamela tells me: "I think you would have the ability to catch me off guard, and that I might be presented with things and experiences I am not used to. I don't think things would look the way I typically see them, as you are very different from the men I have dated. You're from Europe, had a completely different upbringing, have never been married, and have no kids, I think that maybe in the dream I am not sad or overly happy."

That is the dream's prediction based on the current moment. The dream doesn't tell you what to do; therefore you have free will. You need to make a decision based on the information you are given and what works for you. The dream paints the scenario for the future based on the current situation. You decide.

However, things can change, and if the position of each of the people changes, it might change the outcome.

This dream gives a good example of the importance of the experience in the dream, and how to look at the structure and especially take into account the emotions and feelings of the dreamer.

The first part of the work on the dream incubation dream is to look at what the experience is, and figure out the structure or pattern of the dream, and the feelings and emotions. Once that is done, you can read the question against the dream.

Terrell then says, "Machiel, don't leave me hanging. How did it work out with this girl?" I tell him we just left it to that one date.

Step 3: Read the dream against your incubation question

After you have puzzled on the first step—"What is the experience?"—you move to the third step. That is to read your dream response against your incubation question.

The type of question that you ask will give you clues and directions on how to understand your dream response. We will go over the three types of questions—diagnostic/prognostic, request, and prescription—and you will see what I mean.

In working with diagnostic or prognostic dreams

A diagnostic dream gives you a full picture of what is going on, like a dream X-ray.

Prognostic dreams describe the expected outcome. A prognostic dream provides the most likely outcome based on the information in the here and now. Prognostic dreams are not fixed promises that the future will be that way, as there is free will and people continue to make decisions that could influence the initial prognosis. Some tendencies are so far along that they will happen, and others might be bent by free will.

The dream provides you with the best prognosis possible based on what the outcome will be for your question. Then you have the power to decide what to do with the response.

In the Islamic dream incubation tradition, Istakhara, many of the questions posed are prognostic. In fact, Istakhara means to ask Allah to guide one to the right thing concerning any affair in one's life. "What does it look like to marry this person?" and "How will it be for me to enter into a business deal with so and so?" are two such questions.

The interpretation in this ancient and time-proven Islamic tradition is straightforward, and their way can inform our approach. Istakhara looks at whether the experiences in the dream are positive or negative, and certain images can provide clues. If you see anything white (milk, white paper, white clothing, white light, etc.) or green (trees, leaves, vegetables, green fabric, etc.) in your dream, it is considered positive. If you see sacred religious figures or places of peace, the action you are considering is favorable.

If you see the color red, yellow, or black, negative figures that make you fearful or uneasy, or unpleasant experiences, then it is a sign to avoid the situation.

Based on the dream images and experiences that appear, a decision can be made. That makes working with a prognostic dream easier, as you only have to look at positive, neutral, or negative qualities of the dream. You don't need to be a wizard at dream interpretation to understand it. If a person asks whether she should enter into a business deal, and then she sees herself in the dream driving a car that is being attacked by aliens and thus destroyed, she is horrified. Then you don't need to know what the alien means in the dream, or what driving the car means—the dream as a whole just portrays an experience of what that business deal will look like for you. Because the experience is overall negative, the natural answer is not to move forward with the deal.

Terrell's prognosis incubation questions

Terrell says, "All right, let's try those steps on my dream. I created an incubation question that you would call a prognostic question." He continues: "Last year, I had injured my hand with yoga, and I continued to experience pain and strained muscles easily. A friend of mine suggested that I should visit this naturopath he knows. You know, I am always interested in healing traditions and how people do it, plus I wanted to get rid of the pain in my hand. So, on a warm summer day I entered the doctor's office. My doctor was friendly, curious, and focused—maybe even a touch obsessive. He bypassed the formal chitchat and went directly to work. I liked that about him. He used kinesiology, a form of muscle testing, and diagnosed me with several things. For example, he found out that I had mononucleosis when I was a teenager, which is correct, and he said that the mono virus, Epstein-Barr, was currently active. He pushed several times on my stretched arm and decided that I needed to come back four times in two months. At the end of the visit, I walked out with over a hundred dollars in supplements.

"That evening after my doctor's visit I decided to consult the dream about this visit that left some room for skepticism in my mind. Before I went to bed, I asked Dreaming the following prognostic question: 'Dreaming, what do you feel about me continuing to see this doctor?'

"I then had the following dream: 'I see my stepfather. Just as in day-to-day reality, he walks poorly and is not in a great condition. He walks with a cane, and then before my eyes I see him starting to walk better, and his voice becomes strong again. He then walks without help and is quite energetic. I am surprised by this turn of events.'"

"Fascinating dream," I reply, and ask Terrell how he would work with the dream, applying the steps we just went over. To start with, he says, "I ask myself the question, what is the experience?" He muses, "the experience of what is happening is that 'someone who is not in good health and doesn't walk well has a miraculous recovery.' My feeling is that I am surprised, even shocked, by the transformation."

"Now that you have the experience, Terrell, what happens then if you read that against the question of visiting this doctor?" "Well, that is a rather clear sign for me," he says with a grin. "I will continue to see this miracle doctor."

Imani's diagnostic dream

Imani, Terrell's 15-year-old daughter, had asked for a diagnostic dream. She had been struggling with her social life recently. She asked the dream the following question: "What is one of my limiting beliefs that currently hinders me the most?"

Imani says she had the following dream response: "There are several people in conflict, and I am trying to tell them that I am a good person. I am anxiously trying to convince everyone of this by communicating that I am good at figuring out solutions to problems, and therefore have value." There was no resolution in the dream.

We have the lay of the land. Now we need to know the experience, the structure, the dominant emotions, and whether the dream is literal or symbolic.

The structure in this dream is that Imani is trying to prove to other people that she is a good person and has value. She tries to prove that through bringing a solution to people's problems.

Her dominant feelings were of anxiously trying to prove something. By reflecting on it a bit more, she could feel that she was anxious, as she was afraid of not being liked and accepted, and that she wants to be seen as a worthwhile friend.

Then the question is whether this is literal or symbolic. Imani recognizes this literal behavior in her day-to-day life.

The next step in our dreamwork is to read the answer against the question: What is the main limiting belief that hinders me the most right now? Imani now knows what that limiting belief is. The last step is to follow up on her dream. She needs to implement this insight into day-to-day activities. In Imani's case that could start with becoming aware of her tendency to act out this impulse. Only when you become really aware of a limiting belief or harmful behavior can you change it. So she needs to learn how it feels in her body when she does that, and what her thoughts are directly before and when the belief takes hold.

After she has worked on implementing the insights, she could ask for a prescriptive dream such as, "What is one thing I can do to overcome this limiting belief?" or "How can I feel more valuable as a person and a friend?"

Hannah's prescriptive dream question

Hannah had asked for a prescription: "Dreaming, what is a type of food that you recommend I eat regularly?"

Her dream response is as follows: "I am attending a yoga retreat, and I am thinking that I should get back to the practice of daily yoga. Next we are going to have lunch. There is less food on the table than the previous days, but I notice that apart from bread, there are only boiled eggs and peanut butter."

Let's apply the dreamwork guidelines again, starting with the experience.

The dream has two parts, in the first of which Hannah is attending a yoga retreat. I would consider this to be extra advice on the part of the dream. It doesn't really address the food; it addresses her overall health. Yoga is something that Hannah used to do, but due to some injuries, she quit and never got back into it. This is probably literal—the dream is telling Hannah to move her body, either through yoga or other forms of exercise.

In the second part of the dream, there is less food on the table. Hannah says that she had taken that literally. She had noticed that she was slowly eating more in waking life, and that her stomach had adapted to this increased intake.

The eggs and peanut butter, then, could be both literal and symbolic. It could point to some of the nutrients in them, like protein. It could be showing Hannah that she should be eating more healthful foods but not neglect small treats, like the peanut butter. But here lies another opportunity for common sense: for Hannah to begin eating a lot of sugary peanut butter would not be healthy. So if one were to take the dream literally, that is what they would do! Overall, Hannah felt that this was a very clear dream, and was thankful to Dreaming.

The third type of dream is the request, and no one in Terrell's family had asked this particular type of question. Requests are often for an experience or for some help in working through something while asleep. For example: "Dreaming, please help me work through my anger with my friend," or "Dreaming, please help me work through my grief."

What if you don't get a dream?

Tommy was disappointed at the breakfast table and a bit envious; his whole family had gotten guidance and instructive dreams, and he couldn't remember his dream at all! It sometimes happens that we can't remember the dream after an incubation. There are several reasons why that might happen. Yet we will start with the main guideline to take the answer as a response to the incubation question. Therefore, no dream is also an answer. What might such an answer indicate?

The "no dream" as an answer might be reflecting the quality of the question. It may have been a poorly formulated question, it may not have been the right time to know the answer, or it may just be indicating that you need to try asking again.

Sometimes people wake up knowing the answer without remembering the actual dream. In other instances, the answer comes through synchronistic events. I will say more about that shortly. Let's begin with the most common problem.

A poorly formulated question

I asked Terrell how they had handled the lack of dream recall to Tommy's question. Terrell said that they first reviewed his question. Tommy had asked, "Where can I find a suitable job?" The family had questioned whether that was a well-formulated question, and I agree. Terrell thought that Tommy had not really done his homework first. Tommy had been studying for years, yet he didn't know what he wanted to do, or even where he would like to start. The dream doesn't foster co-dependent behavior and figure out for you what you can figure out for yourself. The dream will be more than happy to help as long as you put in effort. In this case, it appears as if the dream might think that Tommy has some introspection to do first—figuring out the different types of jobs out there, the different companies, see what his heart is being drawn to—and then ask the dream for guidance again.

Sometimes the dream question is a good question, but not asked at the right time. Someone might ask where they can find a suitable life partner. Yet it might be that they are first encouraged to work on themselves so that they are really ready to meet the soul mate.

Other times it is just a lack of dream recall. In this case, don't give up. The dream wants you to ask again.

Problem solved—but where's the dream?

It's oft suggested that when you have a problem, sleep on it. The world will usually look different the next day, and you can see situations in a different light.

Johan Cruyff, one of world's best soccer players and arguably the greatest innovator of the game, shared in an interview that he asked for help at night. Johan, who lost his father at a young age, says he still talks to his dad. Cruyff says, "When I have problems, then I usually say before going to sleep, 'Please help me, and then when I wake up tomorrow, I want to know what I have to do.' And then I wake up and I know what I need to do."[5]

Sometimes you will wake up, won't remember the dream, yet you know, in your core, what to do.

No dream remembered, yet the answer comes during the day

Sometimes people have asked me, can the answer come only in a dream? They will often go on to tell me that they got their answer during the day, usually through some synchronistic event, like by reading something in the newspaper or in a conversation with a friend. Someone told me that their eye was drawn to the message on a billboard on the way to work. The Dreaming spirit is active not only during the night but also during the day. It will continue to try to inform you of your sought-after answer, through intuitions and synchronicities (meaningful coincidences). So, yes, you can also get the answer to your dream during the day. And I then tell the people who ask me that question that they are the living proof that the answer can come in many forms, and one is through intuitions and synchronistic events in waking life.

Step 4: Ritual and realization

The last step of the dreamwork is the follow-up phase, the ritual and realization. There needs to be an acknowledgment to the dream that you are thankful for the response, and that you aim to do something with it. The Naskapi Indians, who lived in tune with their dream life, noticed that people who followed up on their dreams would have more dreams and better dreams.[6]

The Asclepeion dream incubation tradition suggested that the god Asclepius appreciated a little token of appreciation. It didn't have to be much, yet something that expressed a sense of gratitude, respect, and relationship. Again, your relationship with the dream is an ongoing friendship.

If you promised to do something, then it is important that you follow through. Implementing the advice is a good way to express gratitude, but doing something extra helps.

The follow-up ritual is important to show gratitude if you got a clear and helpful dream. Yet we also sometimes get a dream that we don't completely understand, and then the follow-up ritual is really important to keep the conversation with the dream going, and testing if the possible interpretation that we made might be the right one. Here is an example of a follow-up ritual on a dream that the asker didn't completely understand. We'll begin with the dream that came as a response to an incubation question posed by Jessy, a member of my dream group.

Question to the dream: "Is there anything I need to talk to my parents about?"

Dream: "I am driving alongside a river. I stop at various places and get out to look around. I keep running into a bear. He's following me. I am interested in the bear and want him to be close, but I'm also afraid of him. I have salmon. I think that's why he's interested in me. I am trying to figure out how to feed the bear without him attacking me, eating me."

There are several possible ways to understand the dream, but let's focus on some ideas for following up on this dream.

The first thing that is an acknowledgment and follow-up: Jessy wrote down the dream and shared it in the dream group.

There are some literal possibilities for follow-up here: He could share the dream question and the dream with his parents. He could make his parents a salmon dinner and tell them the dream. He could make some form of art of the bear and the salmon through drawing, painting, or clay.

These are all activities one can do without understanding the dream, but that will keep the energy of the question alive and will help you figure out what to do over time.

NURTURE YOUR RELATIONSHIP

Working with the dream response can be both challenging and fun. In this chapter we went over four guidelines for working with an incubation dream. Then there is the four-step process of the dreamwork recipe.

This way of working and being with the dream is very much about nurturing a relationship with the "two-million-year-old-man." The goal is to become attentive to what is present, listen with a kind ear to one's own intuition, and have the world of dream infuse your waking reality so that you may live a dream life.

CHAPTER 13

PONDERINGS AND PITFALLS

Maele is drinking coffee, and I sip my South African green tea while we sit in the gentle sun this afternoon in a café in Melville, a suburb of Johannesburg. She is about my age, works for an ad agency in Johannesburg, and is interested in healing and dreams. She grew up in a small village where everybody found it normal to take their dreams seriously. In recent years she had been sitting with the Indigenous healers of her village, deepening her connection to the world of dream and her ancestors. I love learning from her insights, experience, and tradition, and she is curious about the way I approach dreams. We have a conversation about the possible pitfalls of dream incubation.

Does the dream give you an honest answer?

Maele says that the sangoma, the medicine man in her village, always warns of trickster spirits, as they can enter into your dream and trick you. She recounts that someone in her village recently consulted with the dream whether it would be beneficial to enter into a marriage. In the dream this person had seen his ancestors smiling and had taken that as a positive sign. Yet, says Maele, for such a big life question and decision, how can you tell if the dream is being honest or tricking you?

Other people who engage with dream incubation also wonder whether dreams can be trusted, whether they are helpful, and if they guide us in the right direction. If you decide to make major life decisions based on a dream, it is a good thing to ask yourself these questions.

I would be sure to distinguish between regular dreams and the dream response that you get from an incubation. There might be a regular dream in which a trickster pops up, yet if you engage in the sacred activity of connecting with the Mystery, then I do not believe that you will be misguided. If you ask the Mystery a question, I do not believe the dream will purposely trick you or give you the wrong answer. The incubation dream response is aimed at helping you with your life path.

In this way, I think more radically than others. If I ask the dream a question, I work from the premise that the dream responds to it. I believe the sacred connection of asking the Mystery a question cannot be broken. Incubation dreams are, in my opinion, honest and trustworthy.

Dreams are helpful, but do not always tell us what we want to hear.

Dreams can encourage us to become something or warn us not to go in a certain direction. Sometimes, even though those suggestions are helpful to us, we would rather not hear them. Some dreams call us forth into a deeper layer of our own being and ask us to engage with a new activity in our lives. That can sometimes be disturbing, uncomfortable, or scary, despite the fact that this new direction would be wildly positive for us. On top of that, once we do go into the new direction, it is often very enjoyable.

There is an age-old tendency in us humans to refuse the call to adventure. Life invites us to go in a certain direction, yet it doesn't fit with what we have in mind for our own life. We see many of those examples in fairy tales and mythologies of figures that are called to do something and then refuse it, such as the biblical figure of Jonah, who doesn't want to go to Nineveh. Sometimes it is time to leave a relationship, or a job, and we hesitate and wait. Sometimes we have a creative talent such as writing or painting and minimize it and don't really engage with the talent as it would like us to. In those instances, we might get a dream that suggests what to do, but it's something we don't wish to do. It would have been easier to not have the dream, because then we wouldn't have to follow that instruction. Sometimes it is very hard to follow the direction of your life. For example, a spiritually talented woman with a deep love for the practice of yoga asked the dream about her life path. The dream clearly told her that she would benefit from becoming a yoga teacher. However, she wished the dream had not suggested that. She felt initially that she wasn't sure whether she would be a good teacher, whether she had anything to add—and most importantly, she didn't really like the idea of becoming a yoga teacher. She continued to repeat this question several times over the period of a year. Only recently did she follow through upon the call. We all have moments in which we refuse the positive call to become someone or something, for whatever reasons. Sometimes, "It is our light, not our darkness, that most frightens us."[1] Becoming truly ourselves isn't that easy. The dream is honest. It doesn't always tell us what we want to hear, but it tells us what we need to hear.

Other times a dream comes as a warning not to do something we wish for. Sierra, a kind and spirited friend of mine, was looking to buy a house. Just before the housing crash in 2008 she had bought a house, and due to her marriage ending and the bad economic times, she was forced to sell, and on the low end of the market. She is now looking for another house but is finding it hard to find something that both suits her modest needs and is in her price range. She has been following daily e-mail notifications of the houses that are coming on the market, and a couple of times she had been doubting whether she would purchase a certain house. It was never an ideal fit, yet with her purchasing power she realized that it would never be. Once again, a decent little house came on the market, and she wanted to make an offer. Yet she decided first to ask the dream for guidance as to whether this would be a good purchase. She dreamed that she was flying to Paris, a city that breathes joy for her, but the flight toward it was terrible. Then she was a spectator and saw the plane crashing. Sierra said that even more than the dream images, the feeling she had after having this dream was one that gave her the sense that she shouldn't pursue this house. Sierra was disappointed, but intelligently decided to let this opportunity pass.

This is another variation of how dreams are helpful, but they don't always tell us what we want to hear.

Engaging in dream incubation doesn't mean the end of suffering.

Maele says that the path of becoming and being a sangoma is often considered undesirable. They are confronted with illness, have challenging dreams, and need to fight off malicious spirits that try to make their life miserable. The gift isolates a person to a certain extent. Plus, it is sometimes dangerous to deal with dark powers in the Other World.

Incubation dreams help you with your life path and the realization of it, and we could consider that helpful. However, this does not mean that when you are aligned with your path, follow your dreams, and are loyal to life, you will have a life free of trouble and suffering. Living a life connected to your dreams, living a dream life, will not safeguard you against ending up on the cross, so to speak. Jesus did live a life in line with his own path, yet it looks like he didn't see the end coming. He asks in the garden of Gethsemane, "My Father, if it is possible, let this cup pass from me."[2]

Life can sometimes be hard, troublesome, painful, and deeply unfair. These aspects cannot be avoided—one can lose a loved one, experience tremendous heartbreak, or become terminally ill. A proper alignment with the dreams won't prevent that from happening, nor will dream incubation make sure you don't have to face and experience your cross. Yet what dreams can do is help you navigate through and deal with these situations, without the promise that the outcome is what you would like it to be.

Dreams can help us find a stance in which we learn to love the life—including its ups and downs—that has been given to us. They can help us "to joyfully participate in the sorrows of life."[3]

How do I know whether I make the right interpretation?

Maele and I walk from the cozy café to a funky restaurant around the corner. The sun is setting, and it is getting darker. The color of the concrete street is strangely familiar to me. I lived the first four years of my life in South Africa, and when I am back, there is often a sense of deep familiarity with daily life, such as walking in the street, the accents of the people, and the energy of the country. A part of me feels very at ease and at home in South Africa.

While we walk, Maele continues our conversation and ponders my suggestion, that the dream is honest in its response. However, she asks, how do I know whether I am interpreting it correctly? Recently I asked the dream if a certain business direction would be beneficial for me, and then I dreamed that a swarm of bees came to a tree in my yard and started to live in the tree. I thought it was a positive indication, yet how can I know if my interpretation is accurate?

Some dreams are pretty clear, others are more complex, and some are really difficult to understand—you may work the dream, ponder on it, and still have no clue. If you really don't get the dream response, then just ask a follow-up question, or a clarifying question.

There are times we never truly know what the dream response indicates, or whether a decision will work out. Yet we have to go by what we make out of the dream, what our gut tells us, make a decision, and take some risk. Play the game of life. If it then turns out to be a mistake, change your course and figure out how and where you might have misread the dream so that you learn from it. If Maele goes further with her business venture based on her bees in the tree dream, then she must stay attentive. Blind trust is not what is going to serve her, or any of us, at any time. Monitor your decision. You might not be sure about the answer of the dream, but make sure that you participate in the game of life.

Interpretation remains your free will and personal responsibility.

Maele says that the sangomas tell that the ancestors provide help and guidance from the Other World, and that they are on standby to help. Yet due to personal responsibility and free will of the living humans, they can't actively intervene too much in your life, as that might take away from the way you wish to live your life. That is the reason why the ancestors are being asked to help and guide you on a daily basis. It is as if they need to be informed each day about your purpose and goals so that they still know for sure what you want to achieve and can then support you. It is thought that at the end of life, you will be held accountable for your decisions and actions. It won't be the ancestors who will be held responsible for them.

No matter what the dream response is, and what you think it means, you always are personally responsible for the choice you make based on the dream answer you get. Whether you believe that the dream highly encourages you to go in a certain direction, break off a relationship, or purchase a house, it remains your choice and your responsibility. It is even your responsibility whether you make a decision or not, as that is a decision in and of itself.

Your life is always your responsibility, whether you claim this responsibility or outsource it to others such as your parents, boss, scriptures, or God. You make your own decisions, and if your decision is to follow someone else because you think they know better, then that is still your responsibility. If you do something because it is written somewhere, then that is your choice.

You are personally responsible for the actions of your own life. This is the same in the Eastern concept of karma. *Karma* literally means "action," and refers to the idea that actions have consequences, and that the one doing the action will reap the consequence of his action. This consequence can be pleasant or unpleasant. Therefore, in working with the dream response, always remember that you are making the final decision.

This idea of taking personal responsibility for your actions is built into the fabric of life, and also relates to the idea of free will. That means it is up to you, and only you, what you choose. You can choose to swim with the current of life, or against it. We have seen with the woman earlier on that when she would swim against the current, she would feel exhausted and overwhelmed. Yet those are choices that are up to the individual. I have seen instances where people decided to stay with a life partner, despite the fact that the dream suggested there were better options for them.

The African shaman Malidoma Somé told me that in asking the ancestors for help, which is the first line of support in the Other World in the African spiritual tradition, it is fine to ask today for getting help on one thing— getting a job, for example—but if you change your mind the next day, then you ask for what you want again. The ancestors don't mind; they want to help you. You are not locked into a position once you make a decision to go in one direction or the other; free will allows you to change your mind.

In Chapter 4 we discussed the nature of the Mystery, and that it is interested in helping us. The Mystery allows us to choose and is nonjudgmental toward our choices. Naturally there are consequences to your choices, but it is up to you.

Can you attract evil with dream incubation?

Maele says that the sangomas in her village always take great precaution to protect themselves against evil spirits. For example, she says, the Tokoloshe is a spirit that is considered mischievous and evil, and can become invisible by drinking water. Tokoloshes are called upon by malevolent people to cause trouble for others. Wherever I traveled in South Africa, almost everyone knew about the Tokoloshe. There is a considerable fear of these beings. Black magic or witchcraft is very much alive in South Africa, and many people are cautious about it. There are people who actively go to a witch doctor in order to put a curse or a spell on someone else. Maele wonders if people with malicious intentions ask these otherworldly beings for help carrying out their plans.

It is an interesting question from Maele, and I received this particular question multiple times in South Africa. I spoke on dreams at a public lecture organized by the Jungian analysts in Cape Town, where several people in this audience asked me questions about the dangers of attracting or engaging with evil through dream incubation. The same happened in my birth town of Bloemfontein, and in Johannesburg.

This was very interesting to me, as throughout the years this question had not come up in this strong of a way: "Could you use dream incubation for darker purposes, and are we in danger of attracting evil in this way?"

My initial thought was, why would someone want to use it for darker intentions? It would inevitably lead to suffering and pain, as there is such a thing as instant karma. Your own psyche responds directly to your actions and intents. If you start stealing, then you will become more distrustful of others, and perhaps a little more paranoid. You will be less at peace, and access to genuine joy will become difficult. This is a less pleasant way of being in the world, and you can avoid that by not stealing. The same is for any other dark intention and actions; they have a direct effect on your own psyche.

However, if you ask for help with darker intentions, you will receive it. You will attract forces that are malicious, and they will help you with criminal plans, what Indigenous traditions would call "black magic," or any destructive wish you have.

The possible pitfalls of dream incubation.

"You know," says Maele, while she looks at me, "sangomas sometimes lament that the people who visit them don't follow through on their advice and ritual prescriptions, and then the same people return and say that the sangoma's divination doesn't work and that they aren't good healers. I bet you see something like that also in dream incubation, that people don't do anything with the dream suggestions. What are some of the pitfalls that you see with people engaging with dream incubation?"

"Oh yes," I respond, "I have seen people not follow through on the dream suggestion when they have a resistance to their own life path. They might know that they need to end the relationship, or leave their job, yet they don't do it. There is a fear or resistance to venturing into the unknown."

In fact, in my dream groups I have seen that after several weeks people say that they don't want to ask a question because they don't want to know the answer.

There are three other areas of pitfalls I have seen through the years. The first is that people don't understand the dream and then discount the method. The second is more a technical mistake; they don't ask a good question or skip one of the steps of the five-step process. The third is the mentality of the person. They have the wrong attitude, they are lazy or sloppy in the execution of the process, or they forget that dream incubation is really the development of a friendship with the Mystery. Let me explain those three points in a bit more depth.

People don't understand the dream response and then discount the technique.

Sometimes people give up too fast, get a confusing answer, don't puzzle long enough or with sincerity, and then just say it doesn't work. I would like to encourage people to take a bit of time to get acquainted with this method. Take a month—at least—in which you consciously build the relationship with dreaming. In that month, ask several different questions. Get creative. Experiment. That way you can test and verify the method for yourself and embrace a longer-term perspective to learn and grow.

Take care in formulating your question.

The second type of mistake, and the most common mistake, is that people don't ask an alive question and don't formulate the question well. They might also skip one of the other steps from the five-step process. If you are committed to the five steps laid out in this book, you can prevent that mistake from happening.

The mentality toward dreamwork

The third mistake people make has to do with their mentality. They have the wrong attitude, are lazy, or lack discipline. They forget that dream incubation is a friendship with the Mystery, and approach it in the wrong way.

They might also have the wrong attitude toward the dream, and be too arrogant, too impatient, too one-sided.

People can also be a bit sloppy in their approach. Perhaps they don't write down the dream question before they go to bed, change a question without doing the rituals, or postpone writing the dream down in the morning and then only remember half of it.

Ending the evening, and our conversation.

Maele and I are having dinner outside a little restaurant when the power goes out for half an hour. The generator sheds some light inside, and we are sitting with dim lights, candles, and a delicious meal in the warm African summer evening. Asking dreams for help is a journey of explorations; it is about building your own relationship with the Mystery and dreams. One ponders, makes mistakes, learns, and questions possible pitfalls. Along the way, though, one sharpens their technique and nurtures the relationship with care.

AFTERWORD

PLAY THE GAME OF LIFE AND REALIZE YOUR DREAMS

There is help from the world of dream in great abundance. Whether you need help because you are stuck somewhere in your life, need creative inspiration for one of your projects or activities, or wish to heal from an illness, you can realize your desires by asking your dreams for support. This is available to anyone. You don't need any degree, specific upbringing, or anything. Everybody has a relationship to dreams, and dreams are interested in helping you live a fulfilling life.

I hope that you will take this dream technique, experiment and play with it, and make it your own. Develop your own relationship with the world of dream. Engage with your dream, and play the game of life.

That makes me think of a question I once heard: Have you have ever seen people play the game of Monopoly?

Most people have, and what they notice is that those who play the game are really into it. Despite the fact that the game's money is not real money and the properties on the board are not real properties, they can do it for hours. Sitting on the sidelines and watching other people play gets boring quickly. The fun is in participating in the game.

Therefore, participate in the game of life. It doesn't matter whether you "win" or "lose." What matters is that you engage.

Don't wait and wish for so much security from life that you never participate, or only play if you are totally sure that you will win. Because that is actually the only way you can lose the game of life.

Therefore, do not judge yourself on the outcome, but on your participation. Take this dream tool, and play the game of life! Ask as many questions as you like, see what works for you, learn the ways the dream responds to you, be willing to listen, and take action.

YOUR PROBLEMS ARE NOT PERSONAL

The dream loves to help and wants you to live life on your own terms. The dream doesn't mind if you make mistakes or stumble. This is an attitude we should all adopt, as it will help us move through life enjoyably.

In order to find your loved one, improve your finances, be healthier, become a better painter, you will be confronted with areas in your life that aren't going so well. You will be confronted with wounds, problems, and mistakes. The way you look at problems is crucial for the realization of your dreams and your joy in life.

We usually seem to be the most judgmental toward our own mistakes and problems, and we can easily become our own enemy. But there is a better approach: see problems on the road as problems we have, not as problems we are. Then we can engage with the problems in a more detached way, without feeling so bad about ourselves that we construct all kinds of defense mechanisms.

Yet if this self-criticism is something we do struggle with, we can use the dream incubation technique to approach it, and work on the issue until a solution appears.

LIVE A DREAM LIFE

When you embody the insights, wisdom, and creativity of your dreams, you are bringing the dream wisdom and consciousness into your own body and life. You become a vehicle in which the dreamworld can manifest itself and shine through you. You will start to embody your own particular creative spirit, express your own larger wisdom, and be connected to your sense of purpose. You embody the dream consciousness, and in a literal sense, start to live a dream life. Enjoy playing the creative and valuable game of asking your dreams for guidance!

ADDENDUM 1:
AN EMBODIED IMAGINATION
DREAM INCUBATION WITH
ROBERT BOSNAK

Robert Bosnak is a Dutch Jungian analyst and a gifted dreamworker. His main therapeutic style is working with dreams, and he flies all over the world to work with people and their dreams. He has worked with more than 45,000 dreams. He is also one of the few people, or perhaps the only person, who works with dreams and will tell you that he has no idea what dreams mean. That is, he doesn't interpret dreams.

Bosnak developed his own style of working with dreams called "Embodied Imagination." This method is aimed at experiencing the dream rather than interpreting it. In this method, the dreamer uses his or her body to experience the feelings, emotions, and sensations of the dream and the dream figures. Through this technique the dreamer gets an experience of the different states of consciousness in the dream. That is very effective for triggering healing responses or stimulating creativity. The Bosnak method is supported by neuroscience, as it stresses the importance of involving the body and accessing experiences in dealing with psychological problems and the development of creativity. Now Bosnak has schools on four continents where this method is being taught.

I was in my early twenties when I met this dream maverick for the first time. I saw him standing in line for lunch at a Jungian conference in the Netherlands I was attending, and decided to approach him. Several weeks before that conference, I had finished an essay on Jungian psychology and had sent it to Bosnak for feedback. I wanted an experienced Jungian to give me some feedback so I would have an idea of where I was in my journey. Bosnak had said we could talk about it at this conference.

That was the start for me of staying connected and following Bosnak's research on dreams. In my thirties, after I finished my master's in counseling psychology, I followed a three-year training program on Embodied Imagination with Bosnak in Los Angeles. These days, via the educational online organization JungPlatform.com, I facilitate online courses with him.

For this book, I contacted him because I wanted to describe an example of how to do an incubation in his style of Embodied Imagination.

It was also a good time for me to have a serious consult with the dream. I was in a phase where things did not seem to be working out, and I didn't feel at home where I lived. I felt stuck, lonely, tired, and bored out of my mind. In short, it was time to ask the dream for some guidance.

THE INCUBATION

Bosnak and I meet to create the incubation. This dream incubation will not be a formulated question in words, like we explored in this book. I know that in our session Bosnak will search for two or more contrasting states of experiences in a memory or dream. My experience of those two states will function as my incubation.

"You always work on a memory," Bosnak says, "and never on the dream. You work on the memory of the dream."

In the same way you work on a dream, you can work on a memory of a day-to-day experience. Especially if the memory contains part of the problem for which you want to consult the dream. That is what it will be in my case.

I move up and down in my chair while I look at Robert's familiar face. I am hopeful I can consult the dream to deal with this lousy stuckness and boredom. In sinking into the sense of seriousness to consult the dream, I sense a sacredness in turning toward the dream for help. I don't know what will come out of it, but I know that the dream is immensely creative and has a better insight into what is going on, so I am hopeful. I feel like the people who went to the Asclepeion temples; I am working on the incubation with a modern-day Asclepeion dreamworker. It makes me realize more deeply and again that sharing your incubation journey with someone and having them support you is meaningful and helpful, and adds to the incubation experience.

I share with Robert that I feel stuck in my life. For creating this incubation, Bosnak will be less interested in the possible causes of my stuckness; he wants to understand the experience of stuckness that I have.

The first thing Bosnak does is to ask me if I can remember a moment when this stuckness was very strong.

A memory of last Saturday immediately comes to mind. I remember sitting on my couch, bored and lonely. I experience a lack of energy, which feels lousy, as I am well aware that I must do something different to change the situation. However, my energy is so low that that is difficult, and I find almost anything boring, so I am in this lousy cycle. I notice how I try not to be ungrateful and put things a bit more in perspective for myself by stating that I have a house, I am not ill, and I wish that I could just be happy with that. I tell Bosnak that I am not having fun and that I currently don't have an enjoyable life.

Bosnak looks at me, intensely focused, and says, "Yes, feel that . . . feel that you don't have a fun and enjoyable life. Feel what that does to your body." I notice the heaviness in my body.

Bosnak asks where I am when I experience this. I say there was a moment where this experience was very strong—that is last Saturday. I remember, I was sitting on my couch, thinking.

Bosnak asks me, "Are you just fed up?" Oh yes, completely and totally, and I feel just stuck, very stuck. Bosnak continues: "Feel how you are stuck on that couch." Then he starts asking me a series of questions that are aimed at getting me back in that memory, so that I really experience that situation again as if it is happening right now. Bosnak does that by asking specific questions; is it evening, is it still light, are there any sounds, are you drinking something: tea, water, or another drink? After Robert has asked those specific questions: I am completely back in that scene of last Saturday. I can feel how I sit on the couch, see my living room around me, and I feel very well again how I felt in my body.

Bosnak has me experience that deeper: "Feel how you are stuck and that nothing moves. And notice what it does to your body." I feel the energy being sucked out of my body, and I am resisting it. I have been there too much before, and I know that if I live in that sensation, I will become depressed. Bosnak responds, "You are already depressed. One of the definitions of depression is that the energy leaves your body. Where do you feel the energy leave the body?"

I feel it best in my upper legs; it feels like the energy is being sucked out of them. Bosnak then has found a place in my body where I can best experience the emotions and sensations of being stuck, bored, and lacking energy. I stay with that experience for a minute, so I have a deeply embodied experience of it. This is what Bosnak calls an anchor point, a point to anchor the experience so that you can return to it later.

Now that we have the first embodied experience, Bosnak will search for a contrasting state. As I am very much identified with these feelings of being stuck, this contrasting experience is often found in the environment of the memory or the dream. It is often another dream figure, or object.

In order to create the second embodied experience, Bosnak asks me to notice with my back and bump the couch that I am sitting on. How does this couch feel? Is the couch hard or soft?

I sigh, and say that it feels too familiar; I sit there too much. Bosnak wants to see if we can experience the couch itself, and not my feelings toward the couch. Bosnak acknowledges my resistance, and before moving past it, he allows me to sense that resistance for a moment. He says: "Oh, there is boredom . . . again, that couch . . . notice that sensation of 'too much of that couch.'"

Then he tries again to see if we can experience the couch itself. "Sense that couch with your back and buttocks, notice the pillows of the couch, sense the back of the couch—notice the type of material this couch is."

I notice that it is soft and that it is flexible. Bosnak asks if I can sense how flexible that pillow is, and to notice what the substance is like. It is flexible, and yields; Bosnak encourages me to notice what that is like in the couch, that yielding, assimilating, absorbing.

I can sense that it is much more neutral; there is much more flexibility in that. To my surprise, I can notice that the couch itself doesn't feel bored. The couch is flexible, neutral, no hurries, all is fine, and very much in the now. It is all good. I can feel that in my shoulders.

Bosnak says, "Continue to sense the body of the couch in the shoulders—flexible, neutral—and notice where the couch is most aware of that yielding and absorbing."

I can feel that clearly and strongly in the chest and shoulders.

Bosnak says, "Notice, in the chest and shoulders of the couch, that it is the couch, not Machiel. Notice how flexible it is, how it absorbs Machiel."

I can sense how this state is warmer, lighter, easier. Bosnak then creates the second anchor point of the yielding, flexible, absorbing, lighter, warmer couch, and locates that in the shoulders.

Now we have two embodied experiences, and they will be used as the incubation. Robert then has me sit and circle through these two experiences for several minutes.

We finish the incubation session by Robert telling me to practice these two states several times before I go to bed, as a sort of ritual. Then I am to look at my dreams for the next three days. Robert uses three days of dreaming, where I normally only take the one night after the incubation. This is just a way of setting the agreement with the dream. You can experiment and create your own form of communication.

This is an incubation in the style of Embodied Imagination. It doesn't pose a question in words, yet it puts out two or more embodied states and hopes for a response by the dream.

MY RESULTING DREAMS

In my first dream, I walk down a street, and I see on a square to the left my longtime friend from high school times in the Netherlands. I am immediately very happy to see him, and I say hi to him and his wife.

Then I walk with one or two other people into a café, and I see my mother and five of her friends. I am pleasantly surprised to see her. I experience fun and lightness.

In the next scene I walk into the Roxy, a trendy club I went to in the '90s in Amsterdam. I feel ecstatic, as I am with fun friends, in a stylish club with great music where I know there are often interesting people, and I might even meet a possible future girlfriend. My friend orders four tequila shots, and I drink one with him.

I wake up and know that what I dreamed about was what I miss: good friends, laughing, trendy places, the chance to meet a fitting partner. I stay close to the experience of the dream and feel the joy, the love, the ecstasy for life. While I lie in bed, I let that sense of love for life infuse my overall lousy state.

The next night I fly to the Netherlands and don't remember the dream I have sleeping in the airplane, but the third night I have the following dream experience: "I am having a conversation with a woman I had just met that day in Amsterdam and another man who is a well-known person in the Jungian world. I am talking about the limiting self. And they propose that I stay and explain more about the limiting self. In the next scene, I am in a university building, I am on stage, and there is an audience. I know I am to do a psychological riff, a form of improv on a psychological concept, on this concept of the limiting self. I feel a bit intimidated. Then I just start talking. 'In working with the limiting self, the great art is of letting go, and then everything, everything becomes alive.'"

Therefore, I focus on being more spontaneous to break out of my limiting self and constricting feelings of depression.

I work with Robert Bosnak on these dreams again through the Embodied Imagination style, in which we explore different states, the sense of the limiting self, and the spontaneity of riffing. This all contributed to working through that lousy phase, and months later I am fully back on track, focused, passionately engaged with my life. The incubation work with Bosnak has been a positive force in my working through that experience.

You could play with this method and go to a feeling state; see if you can sense that in your body, and then use that for an incubation.

ADDENDUM 2: QUESTIONS TO ASK THE DREAM

Love / Relationships

- How do I develop a secure attachment?
- Can you, Dream, show me my abandoned self?
- What can I do to find my soul mate?
- How can I become a trap for love (Rumi)?
- How can I be more vulnerable in my love life?
- How can I resolve my feelings with my father (or mother, or boss, or partner)?
- What is a behavior in me that prevents me from finding a partner?
- To figure out what is really going on in your relationship, you can ask the question, "What is the situation between me and person x?"
- How can I love my partner better?

Life Path

- What do I need to focus on most right now?
- Dreaming, can you show me something that is important for me to see and/or know?

- In my dream tonight, clearly explain to me how I can find my life's purpose.

- Please show me the blind spot in my life that is currently hindering me the most.

Personal Growth

- What is the source of my anger?

- What is the reason for my failing in a particular endeavor?

- While I am sleeping, can you help me work through my issue with (grief, anger, patience, my partner)?

- Which one of my limiting beliefs is hindering me most right now? And as a follow-up: How do I overcome this limiting belief?

Health

- What is one type of food that you recommend I add or continue to have in my diet?

- What is one type of food that you recommend I remove from my diet?

- How can I improve my health?

- What daily activities can I do to live a healthier life?

Finances, Worth, and Self-Value

- What kind of value do I place on my financial worth?

- What is one thing I can do to increase my self-worth?

- What will make me feel rich?

- How do I develop healthy generosity?

- What does money mean to me?

- What is one thing I need to know about my unconscious belief about money?

- What is one obstacle in my belief toward money?

Spiritual Explorations

- Ask to meet a dead relative.

- Ask a dead relative if they have a message for you.

- What will it be like when I have passed on?

- I would like to meet my spirit guide.

- How can I build a relationship with my spirit guide?

- Help me understand a philosophical concept (after you tried your best to understand it). For example: What is a life contract? What is the life review? What is karma?

- What is the purpose of the Universe?

- Please permit me to see what I do at night during astral travels.

Creativity

- For a book, what could this character do right now?
- How can I improve my painting or drawing skills?
- Please provide an image that I could paint at this moment.
- If you have a business and want to grow it: How do I get more clients who would benefit from my services?

Fun

- I would like a joyful dream to lift my spirits.
- I would like to laugh in my dream tonight.
- What would be a good activity for me to engage in that would help me to experience more fun in my life?
- Please show me a way to look at life that makes me laugh more and see the humor of a situation.
- How can I laugh about myself more?

Nightmares

- Monster, do you have a message for me?
- Chaser, is there something you want from me?
- How can I better deal with my anxiety about (insert topic of the dream)?

ENDNOTES

Chapter 3

1. "When Gandhi Dreamed of Resistance: The Committee in Non-Western Cultures." https://www.mkgandhi.org/autobio/chap154.htm

2. A. McCoy, and Y. Siang, "Otto Loewi (1873–1961): Dreamer and Nobel Laureate," *Singapore Medical Journal* 55(1) (January 2014): 3–4. http://www.ncbi.nlm.nih.gov/pmc/articles/PMC4291908.

3. Sonu Shamdasani, editor, *Introduction to Jungian Psychology* (Princeton, Princeton University Press, 2011), 25.

Chapter 4

1. *The Holy Bible English Standard Version* (2016), Matthew 7:7.

2. *Quran* 40:60.

3. Marie-Louise von Franz, *Archetypal Dimensions of the Psyche* (Boston: Shambhala, 1999), 293.

4. Patrick Harpur, *The Secret Tradition of the Soul* (Berkeley: North Atlantic Books, 2011), 91–92.

5. Michael Meade, *The Genius Myth* (Housatonic, MA: Green Fire Press, 2016).

6. C. G. Jung, trans. Richard and Clara Winston, *Carl Jung's Memories, Dreams, Reflections* (New York: Vintage Books, 1989), 413, 418.

7. Patrick Harpur, *Daimonic Reality: A Field Guide to the Otherworld* (Enumclaw, WA: Pine Winds Press, 2003).

8. James Hillman, *The Soul's Code* (New York: Ballantine Books, 2017), 39–40.

9. James Hillman, *The Soul's Code* (New York: Ballantine Books, 2017), 39–40.

10. C. G. Jung, trans. Richard and Clara Winston, *Carl Jung's Memories, Dreams, Reflections* (New York: Vintage Books, 1989), 413, 418.

11. Steve Jobs, Stanford Commencement Address, June 2, 2005, https://www.youtube.com/watch?v=UF8uR6Z6KLc.

12. Patrick Harpur, *The Secret Tradition of the Soul* (Berkeley: North Atlantic Books, 2011), 112.

Chapter 5

1. Joan C. Hartan, *Working the Day Shift: Using Dream Incubation to Change Your Life* (Createspace Independent Publishing Platform, 2014), 33, 34.

2. Iain R. Edgar, *The Dream in Islam: From Qur'anic Tradition to Jihadist Inspiration* (New York: Berghahn Books, 2016), 42, 45.

3. Kelly Bulkeley, *Dreaming in the World's Religions: A Comparative History* (New York: New York University Press, 2008), 108.

4. Meredith Sabini, "Incubated Dreaming: A Natural Spiritual Instinct," *Dream Time* 1, No. 3 (Winter 2004), 20–21. http://dream-institute.org/wp-content/uploads/21.3_WI04 _DreamTime_Sabini.pdf.

5. Jordan Lite, "How Can You Control Your Dreams?" *Scientific American,* July 29, 2010, http://www.scientificamerican.com/ article/how-to-control-dreams.

6. Deirdre Barrett, "The 'Committee of Sleep': A Study of Dream Incubation for Problem Solving," *Dreaming* 3, No. 2 (1993). http://www.asdreams.org/journal/articles/barrett3-2.htm.

Chapter 6

1. C. G. Jung, trans. Richard and Clara Winston, *Carl Jung's Memories, Dreams, Reflections* (New York: Vintage Books, 1989), 192–193.

Chapter 7

1. Emma Jung and Marie-Louise von Franz, *The Grail Legend* (Princeton: Princeton University Press, 1998), 295.

2. Robert A. Johnson, *He: Understanding Masculine Psychology,* (New York: Perennial Library, 2020), 11, 79.

Chapter 9

1. TEDxMileHigh, "How to Ask Better Questions," July 17, 2015, https://www.youtube.com/watch?v=J8xfuCcXZu8&feature= youtu.be.

2. Robert Waggoner, *Lucid Dreaming: Gateway to the Inner Self* (Needham, MA: Moment Point Press, 2008), 141.

3. Lelyveld, *How Questions Affect Answers* (October 5, 1986,) 65–76. https://courses.eller.arizona.edu/mgmt/delaney/p_chapter6.pdf.

Chapter 10

1. Robert Waggoner, *Lucid Dreaming: Gateway to the Inner Self* (Needham, MA: Moment Point Press, 2008), 109–125.

2. Kelly Bulkeley, *Dreaming in the World's Religions: A Comparative History* (New York: New York University Press, 2008), 31.

3. Robert Bosnak, "Inviting Creative Genius into Your Life: Class 2," https://jungplatform.com/store/invite-creative-genius-into-your-life.

4. Emma Edelstein and Ludwig Edelstein, *Asclepius: Collection and Interpretation of the Testimonies* (Baltimore: The Johns Hopkins University Press, 1988), 188, 190.

Chapter 12

1. Judith Harris, editor, *The Quotable Jung* (Princeton, New Jersey: Princeton University Press, 2015), 70, 71, 74.

2. C. G. Jung, *The Red Book: Liber Novus (New York: W. W. Norton & Company, 2009).*

3. Robert Waggoner, *Lucid Dreaming: Gateway to the Inner Self* (Needham, MA: Moment Point Press, 2008).

4. Jolande Jacobi, editor, C. G. Jung: *Psychological Reflections (Princeton: Princeton University Press, 1973).*

5. Interview on *De Wandeling* with Sander de Kramer, 2015.

6. C. G. Jung, *Man and His Symbols* (New York: Dell Publishing, 1968), 161.

Chapter 13

1. Marianne Williamson, *A Return to Love: Reflections on the Principles of A Course in Miracles* (New York: HarperOne, 1996).

2. *The Holy Bible*, The King James Version, Matthew 26:39.

3. Friedrich Nietzsche, *The Gay Science: With a Prelude in Rhymes and an Appendix of Songs* (New York: Vintage Books, 1974).

ACKNOWLEDGMENTS

As many know—and as one often reads in these acknowledgments—a book is not a solo project, despite the fact that it shows up on the shelf with just the name of the author on it. I am grateful for all of those helping hands and supporting minds that I have encountered and journeyed with on the way to bringing this book into the world.

Naturally, I need to acknowledge that I am part of a long tradition of people who have asked the world of dream and its inhabitants for guidance, and who have gotten help. Many known and unknown people have contributed to the development of my ideas and technique.

I am deeply grateful to Hay House for believing in this book. A special heartfelt thanks goes out to the following Hay House team members: My friendly and gifted editor, Anna Cooperberg, who helped me sharpen and beautify the manuscript; Patty Gift, Allison Janice, Celeste Johnson, Karim Garcia, Nick Welsh, Devon Glenn, Micah Kandros, Brianne Bardusch, and Tania Bissell.

Susan Mann has given me input and encouragement during the creation of this book. When I doubted myself, she gave me the confidence I needed, and assured me that I was working on a meaningful endeavor.

One of my most beloved companions on the road of life is my sister Akke-Jeanne, and she has provided many valuable and interesting insights on the book, and made the journey so much more fun. I also want to thank my dear friend Andrew Harvey for his support.

I admire the exceptional dreamworkers Robert Bosnak and Robert Waggoner, and thank them for reading my manuscript and providing helpful input.

Many thanks to all the dreamers who have participated in my dream groups, shared dreams, and taken part in experiments. Among them is my mother, Ank van der Woude.

Valuable friends—including my Dutch friends Gerland Slump and Taco van der Mark, and dream friends such as Lynda St. Dennis, Cherella Forester, Laura Pritchett, Katy Cook, Johan van der Walt, and the magical dreamer Jamie Watkins—have been there with me the entire way. Finally, I want to thank Monica Dennis for sharing dreams and her ongoing encouragement and support.

ABOUT THE AUTHOR

Machiel Klerk is a licensed mental health therapist, international speaker, dreamworker, author and social entrepreneur.

He has been a mental health therapist since 2006, and currently has an online private practice. While obtaining a master's degree in counselling psychology at Pacifica Graduate Institute, he studied Jungian psychology. Fascinated by healing traditions, he has travelled all over the world and studied many cultures and their healing and dream technologies – specifically African traditions, as he was born in South Africa. He grew up in the Netherlands, and currently resides in the United States.

Machiel has given lectures and workshops throughout Europe, South Africa and North America about dreams and psychology. He also provides inspirational talks and workshops for companies on creativity, innovation and leadership. He has written several articles on dreams and released a course on the Jung Platform.

Machiel has vocationally been guided by dreams when he founded the Jung Society of Utah and the online organization Jung Platform because of a nighttime dream. In appreciation for these contributions, he has received several awards from the local community.

www.MachielKlerk.com

Hay House Titles of Related Interest

Hay House Podcasts
Bring Fresh, Free Inspiration Each Week!

Hay House proudly offers a selection of life-changing audio content via our most popular podcasts!

Hay House Meditations Podcast

Features your favorite Hay House authors guiding you through meditations designed to help you relax and rejuvenate. Take their words into your soul and cruise through the week!

Dr. Wayne W. Dyer Podcast

Discover the timeless wisdom of Dr. Wayne W. Dyer, world-renowned spiritual teacher and affectionately known as "the father of motivation." Each week brings some of the best selections from the 10-year span of Dr. Dyer's talk show on Hay House Radio.

Hay House Podcast

Enjoy a selection of insightful and inspiring lectures from Hay House Live events, listen to some of the best moments from previous Hay House Radio episodes, and tune in for exclusive interviews and behind-the-scenes audio segments featuring leading experts in the fields of alternative health, self-development, intuitive medicine, success, and more! Get motivated to live your best life possible by subscribing to the free Hay House Podcast.

Find Hay House podcasts on iTunes, or visit www.HayHouse.com/podcasts for more info.

CONNECT WITH
HAY HOUSE
ONLINE

🌐 hayhouse.co.uk   f @hayhouse

📷 @hayhouseuk   🐦 @hayhouseuk

▶ @hayhouseuk   ♪ @hayhouseuk

Find out all about our latest books & card decks • Be the first
to know about exclusive discounts • Interact with our authors
in live broadcasts • Celebrate the cycle of the seasons with us
• Watch free videos from your favourite authors •
Connect with like-minded souls

'The gateways to wisdom and knowledge
are always open.'

Louise Hay